W

More than seventy years after an imposing church-warden declared, 'The laddie must join the choir,' Reg Frary still sings in his parish church choir in Richmond, Surrey.

Here he has found ample inspiration for his affectionate and amusing stories of passion and intrigue beneath the cassocks, which a loyal following of readers has enjoyed for more than forty years.

This is Reg Frary's third collection of choir tales to be published by the Canterbury Press.

What a Performance

More sweet singing (well . . . singing)
from the choir

Reginald Frary

CANTERBURY
PRESS
Norwich

Text © Reginald Frary 2004

First published in 2004 by the Canterbury Press Norwich
(a publishing imprint of Hymns Ancient & Modern Limited,
a registered charity)
St Mary's Works, St Mary's Plain,
Norwich, Norfolk, NR3 3BH

www.scm-canterburypress.co.uk

British Library Cataloguing in Publication data

A catalogue record for this book is available
from the British Library

ISBN 1-85311-589-4

Typeset by Rowland Phototypesetting Limited,
Bury St Edmunds, Suffolk
Printed and bound in Great Britain by
Bookmarque, Croydon, Surrey

Contents

Dedication

To my friend Eve Hunt and her 'confederates' in the choir of St Mary Magdalene, Crowmarsh Gifford, Oxfordshire.

Preface

When I was a choirboy and took the words of some of our great Christian hymns more literally I often used to wonder about those heavenly choirs, so often referred to, who sing gloriously day and night for ever and ever.

In our choir, particularly on cold, soaking wet, November Sunday evenings when the organist was rapidly growing purple in the face because the organ was 'acting up' once again, the vicar had changed the tune of his favourite hymn, half the choirboys were absent with very sudden colds or queasy stomachs and the bass who always sang half a tone below everyone else was on absolutely buoyant form, we had an awful job just getting through an hour of choral evensong, let alone singing celestially ad infinitum . . .

Reg Frary

A Fashionable Episode

The elegant southern town where my friend Roger is director of music at the church is one of a select few that years ago were known as fashionable. The residents, the shops, the health club, the golf club were all fashionable. The church at its centre was fashionable. It was built by a famous fashionable architect towards the end of the nineteenth century and Roger's grandmother always referred to it as catering for 'carriage trade'. It was the 'daughter' church to the parish church, an ancient soot-blackened pile that sprawled near the rusting railway goods yards at the edge of the town and wasn't fashionable at all. Roger's grandmother said it had a dreadful, loud choir whose favourite hymn seemed to be 'The Battle Hymn of the Republic' which they sang at every available opportunity including Christmas and weddings and baptisms. She said the choir was full of engine drivers and shunters who all rolled straight into the Railway Arms after Sunday matins. Roger reckoned his grandmother delighted in shuddering every time anyone mentioned the parish church choir . . .

Today, happily, both churches are still alive and well. No one now uses the word fashionable referring to the daughter church, which is now a separate parish church, although I know that Roger still feels that his choir is fashionable and the old parish church choir remains as affectionately dreadful as ever.

But, apart from the choir, everything in Roger's church has changed now. The present vicar is a modern, progressive young woman whose enthusiasm for changing everything that prevailed in the church before she arrived, and for centuries before that, is only slightly curbed by stalwarts like Edie the retired schoolmistress, a highly respected lady with blue hair who occupies a back pew near the main entrance to the church and regularly castigates members of the congregation who turn up late for the services or steal a crafty nap during the sermon (they say she keeps lists). As well as being highly respected Edie is a very important parish figure, for she it is who edits the parish magazine. This means she picks up any parishioners' notes that drop through her letter box, paper-clips them together and takes them round to a retired gentleman who does a bit of home printing as a hobby. Always anxious to cram as much good news as possible into the magazine, he happily dispenses with all paragraphing and most punctuation, including apostrophes (except when he puts apostrophes where they shouldn't be), the result each month being a dozen pages of dense print headed by the bold words *Hi, everyone!* over a photo of the vicar wearing a T-shirt sporting a large photo of a scowling pop group. Beneath this there is always a notice drawing attention to a toddlers' group next to an advertisement for a firm that carries out dignified funerals at the cheapest rates for miles.

Thus for years the parish magazine has appeared, and, until recently, been tolerated in a true Christian spirit as a sort of revered parish tradition, drawing neither condemnation nor praise from the parishioners, even though some of them do manage to decipher most of the text most of the time.

Then there occurred the clerical blunder that shook the tradition. The vicar, noting a more than usual drop in the number of choir members, through natural causes, had, without recourse to editor Edie and her paper clip or musical director Roger, inserted a large notice at the end of the magazine: 'Wanted – singers for our choir. Come along and enjoy yourselves. No experience necessary!'

Roger was furious – even more furious than at the annual combined churches Ascension Day choral evensong when his choir were traditionally

3

obliged to sing with the parish church choir who, he accused, regularly drowned his choir's beautiful tones with 'a display of raw brute force and ignorance' in the performing of Gounod's 'Unfold Ye Portals Everlasting'.

'How dare she!' he piped. What did she think she was doing? Openly inviting people with no experience of music or singing to join the choir – *his* choir, who year after year won top place in the choirs section of the local music festival and sang at all the fashionable weddings. 'Can you imagine the kind of characters we shall get trying to join our choir now?' he fumed. 'People who can't read music and who can't even *begin* to appreciate Vivaldi – the types who just want to bawl lots of alleluias, strum guitars and clap.'

'Sounds awful,' I sympathized.

'These people have been waiting in the wings for years,' claimed Roger darkly.

'You'd think they'd have got themselves into the parish church choir,' I suggested.

'Good heavens, not a chance down there,' he said. 'To give that parish church lot their due, they wouldn't have any truck with guitars and clapping. They haven't moved anywhere since the middle of the nineteenth century. They're sticking to the first edition of *Hymns Ancient & Modern* and full organ.'

But Roger need not have worried. The vicar's

invitation to members of the congregation to join the choir produced no new choristers. In a vague way the congregation were proud of their prize-winning choir and enjoyed their music week by week. They liked listening but drew the line at the prospect of giving up hours and hours regularly, learning from Roger the right way to sing Vivaldi, how to appreciate Bruckner and the correct pronunciation of Latin passages. Joining in some good sturdy singing of popular hymns in the Sunday morning congregation gave them all the inspiration they needed.

Nevertheless, the vicar's invitation did get one or two people thinking – but not thinking so loftily that they entertained thoughts of possible membership of Roger's exclusive band of singers. They thought they might be all right in the parish church choir, where they could sing even more sturdily than in the congregation at Roger's church. So down at the parish church they dug out some more veteran hymn books, and the volume of boisterous praise in that ancient place increased.

The bright young vicar of Roger's church was quick to realize the serious error of her ways in appealing for new members for the choir without consulting anyone. You just don't ride roughshod over highly respected parish magazine editors and conductors of fashionable, prize-winning choirs and drive members of your congregation into the arms of inferior set-ups like the parish church choir. As Roger sought to impress on his wife, a down-to-earth, quite unmusical lady who couldn't understand what all the fuss was about, 'That's simply not the correct way to treat people, it's not the way to do things.'

'You and that choir lot are like a gang of squabbling kids,' declared his wife. 'You all get together in the choir vestry and do your warbling and tell each other how good you are, and then get upset when people don't realize it. You're not happy unless you're tearing someone to bits.'

'We're defending our traditions of fine church music,' began Roger.

'Traditions, my foot,' broke in his wife. 'You're just a bunch of people with delusions of grandeur. Hurry up and eat your porridge. It'll be cold and you'll be late for the family service.'

Meanwhile, life at the parish church had indeed not changed. The vicar, a very popular old bachelor, had been there for years, knew everyone by their Christian names, preached sermons that everyone wanted to hear, chose the right hymns and joined the choir in the Railway Arms every Sunday after evensong. Who wanted change?

But outside the parish church change was rampant. In the course of 'modernizing' the railways –

depriving people of local lines, closing freight depots, running fewer trains, charging increased fares for a poorer service and forcing even more traffic on to the choked roads – the area around the parish church was becoming transformed. Most of the old goods yards and buildings were being swept away and an up-to-the-minute upgraded look was being developed in the shape of new concrete and glass blocks of offices with extensive car parks, and little public parks whose main object seemed to be to ban dogs. In the face of this great enlightening clean-up it was thought necessary that the parish church should also be cleaned up to blend in with the general scheme. Scaffolding suddenly enmeshed the venerable pile, both without and within, making it necessary to close the church temporarily for the first time in 200 years – not that the place (except the choir vestry) had not been redecorated in all that time, but now a very big operation was in hand. And once again the lady vicar's youthful naivety was blatantly demonstrated when in a spirit of Christian togetherness, she invited the parish church choir to join Roger's choir for the Sunday services while their church was unavailable.

On the morning of the first 'combined choir' family service at Roger's church I was fulfilling a long-standing invitation to sing in his choir and we now stood together in the sunny churchyard as we awaited the dreadful advent of the parish church choir.

'This is going to be a disaster,' Roger groaned for the umpteenth time. He had spent a long, sleepless nightmare of a night trying to visualize exactly what kind of a disaster awaited him and his singers at the hands of the parish church choir, who outnumbered his choir three to one and sang everything at full volume. 'Submerged, we shall be,' he groaned, 'totally submerged.'

I didn't quite know what to say. 'Perhaps they will let up a bit,' I ventured, unconvincingly. Roger ignored the remark, as unworthy of comment I suppose, but then suddenly his mood lightened as something like relief calmed his expression.

'Wait a minute,' he said. 'Things may not be quite so bad.'

Apparently, in keeping with advanced theory, the lady vicar fervently believed that at the family service all members should sit, kneel, stand and sing together as 'one joyous, indivisible family', and the choir should not be distanced behind the chancel screen up in the choir stalls dressed in outmoded, alienating robes. Consequently, Roger's choir these days sat in the first rows of the congregation, dressed normally, and the choir stalls remained empty.

'The parish church lot won't stand for any

mucking about with the choir like that,' Roger assured me eagerly. 'They always wear cassocks and surplices and sit well away from the congregation in the choir stalls. They read the Sunday papers during the sermon and do crosswords. They couldn't do that sitting in the congregation. They'll insist on sitting in the choir stalls, Sunday papers and all. We can get rid of them up there!'

'You see, there's always hope,' I said, 'even in the darkest moments.'

'We'll only have to put up with them joining in the hymns,' he enthused, 'and they will have to sit down and listen when we sing the Vivaldi.'

'They'll probably be doing their crosswords,' I said.

He nodded. 'It could be not so bad after all.'

Presently, half a dozen assorted cars and trucks pulled up outside the churchyard and the parish church choir trooped out, with cassocks, surplices and wads of Sunday papers. They were greeted glowingly by the lady vicar and a shade less glowingly by Roger. The vicar engagingly explained about the joyous indivisibility family service policy now practised at the church but, to Roger's great relief, soon gave up when the parish church choir, despite listening politely, proceeded to robe and sort out their places in the choir stalls.

Consequently the service was soon ready to commence, with the two choirs in separate parts of the church. And in the circumstances this was fortunate indeed, as it would have been most inconvenient to accommodate the parish church choir in the congregation, owing to the presence there of dozens of visiting American conference visitors who filled every spare pew space and window ledge. So, preceded by a sparkling speech of welcome to the parish church choir all about dedicated, distinguished musicians (the parish church choir had never been called anything like that before and wondered what she was talking about) the service got under way.

Everyone listened respectfully – and some with serene joy – to the Vivaldi, performed peerlessly by Roger's choir, who were joined enthusiastically by the parish church choir (who could be heard hugely despite being up in the choir stalls) in the singing of the hymns. At the end of the service, as a tribute to the many American visitors present, the vicar announced that they would finish with 'The Battle Hymn of the Republic' – 'Mine eyes have seen the glory of the coming of the Lord'. There arose the loudest volume of sound I had heard in a church for many a day. We sang every verse. On a glorious English summer morning, with the church flooded with sunlight and bedecked with flowers, we sang Julia Ward Howe's words straight from a Union army camp in the American Civil War:

I have seen Him in the watchfires of a
    hundred circling camps;
They have builded Him an altar in the evening
    dews and damps;
I have read His righteous sentence by the dim
    and flaring lamps;
His day is marching on.

Even Roger's choir looked as though they were
enjoying themselves . . .

The parish church choir are now back in their
splendidly refurbished church and carrying on as
ever. Roger says he is working on an exciting
arrangement of 'The Battle Hymn of the Republic'
as a meditative quartet with flute accompaniment.
It is far beyond my limited musical comprehension
to imagine how he will do this – but do it he will.
Then it will be acceptable for a fashionable choir
to sing.

2

What a Performance

'There's this new woman in our matins congregation who says she's an opera singer,' explained my friend Hacksaw (the village organist and choirmaster of whom I have written many times before). 'She sits at the back of the church and warbles very, *very* loudly and upsets the whole congregation – completely disorientates them. There's going to be trouble, I can tell you.'

'I can well believe it,' I said. 'It must be awful for them. Your congregation don't sing at all, do they, never have done. It must be most disturbing to have a loud person like this new lady among them.'

'Exactly!' agreed Hacksaw. 'There's always been a serene, peaceful atmosphere in the congregation at choral matins. They rely on the choir to do any singing – and we don't disturb them much, of course, because we're tucked well away from them behind the choir screen.'

'And what a screen!' I enthused.

'Yes,' he agreed proudly. 'People come for miles to see it, you know – fifteenth century, solid oak floor to ceiling and weighs five tons.'

'A rare treasure,' I said.

'Indeed,' he smiled, 'and it makes it so much easier for the choir to ignore the sermon altogether after they've already picked up muffled snatches of the *same* sermon through the oak every few weeks.'

I've often thought that Hacksaw really should try his hand at scripting some episodes for television soap operas. He would be great! Whenever I happen to drop in on him and sing in his choir he's always ready with detailed updates of the latest intriguing situations fermenting in the parish, situations, it has to be said, welcomed enthusiastically by the lovely new, trusting, young lady vicar as thrilling evidence that her parishioners are now actively thinking, questioning and discussing their church, not just meekly accepting moribund traditional notions. Hacksaw's reports of parish thinking, questioning and discussing on the subject of the intrusive opera singer in the matins congregation appealed immediately to my sense of suspense. How could anyone dare to walk into a church and threaten age-old revered traditions, like no one ever singing at choral matins, and expect to get away with it? The idea was monstrous.

On Sunday morning Hacksaw and I arrived early

at the church for the service. A large, dark-grey suited sidesman with a formidable expression and very shiny shoes was already on duty at the door, handing out hymn books together with colourful weekly parish news leaflets, lately introduced by the new lady vicar, that always opened with the words *Hi there, folks* . . . Hacksaw explained that this was the vicar's effort to try to dilute the strictly formal atmosphere at matins and gently persuade the congregation that they were part of the parish family who attended the happy-go-lucky-anything-goes family service that followed matins.

'Not that this ruse has any effect on our congregation,' he asserted. Quite expectedly, they still politely addressed the lady as 'vicar', and not as 'Bertha' or 'Young Bert', and had nothing to do with the kind of hullabaloo that erupted at the back of the church after the family service.

Another old friend, the choir's bass soloist, joined us. 'It's like this, you see,' he clarified. 'The vicar reckons that people who come to the service should end up all joyous afterwards.'

'Well, our matins lot are not exactly *miserable*,' defended Hacksaw. 'Dignified, but not miserable.'

'Granted,' agreed the bass, 'but the absence of misery doesn't automatically mean you're joyous – especially not that "ten-minute sermon limit" crowd who sit under the pulpit with stopwatches.'

'Well, they would be joyous if the vicar got the sermon finished in ten minutes, but she never does, so what can you expect?' asked Hacksaw.

As we robed in the vestry the new vicar strode in pushing her blue and gold mountain bike and trilling, 'Hi there, everyone! What a glorious morning.' In the next few minutes she had parked the bike precariously across a wobbly umbrella stand, clipped on her plastic clerical collar and come to the rescue of the local football team who were being roundly reviled by three senior choirmen for losing the Saturday match for the seventh time in succession.

'Come on now, you lot,' she intervened vigorously. 'It was just a bit of bad luck, that's all. It could happen to any of us. We've got a grand team here, chaps. Just give them a little time.'

The 'chaps' regarded her speechlessly and she beamed encouragingly at us all as we formed up and trailed into church to begin the service.

Slightly muted though it was by the famous church screen's tons of oak, the confident screech from the rear of the congregation, like unto a distressed police car siren, soon hit the choir during the first hymn. 'She's flat again,' mumbled the bass soloist to me as we finished.

'So were we,' responded a soprano in front of us, a blatantly attractive young woman who sang most of the soprano solos because Hacksaw, a showman at heart, considered she added tone to the appearance of the choir. 'We're always flat in "Through the Night of Doubt and Sorrow".'

'Yes, but she was flatter,' insisted the bass. 'I say! I've just had a terrible thought!'

The call for our musical services precluded the revelation of the bass's terrible thought until we reached the sermon. Then the choristers nearest him moved closer, keen to learn the worst. The bass soloist often had terrible thoughts about the parishioners and they were always intriguingly startling in a negative sort of way.

'What if the vicar invites her to join the choir?' he whispered hoarsely. 'The vicar's always going on about us having too few ladies in the choir compared with all our men.'

'She's right in a way,' put in the soprano, 'but not *that* right.' Her pretty face became a mask of horror. 'We can't have *her* up here!'

The bass glanced down at the rows of the stony-faced congregation. 'They're not listening to the sermon,' he said. 'They're *seething* – absolutely *seething*. Oh yes, you can see it coming – we're going to get lumbered with her.'

'We can speak to the vicar, sort of firmly,' suggested the soprano.

'Won't do any good,' assured the bass. 'It'll be all

girls together with that one. She'll welcome her into the choir with open arms and her special joyous smile – she never fails with her special joyous smile . . .'

After the sermon, which the vicar, aware of the presence of the stopwatch vigil below the pulpit, triumphantly bawled through in ten minutes flat, the rest of the service was conducted at a rollicking pace and we were soon moving towards the coffee room, a coal-cellar-like area in the crypt decorated with large crayon drawings produced by Sunday school pupils, depicting prehistoric monsters and their new superintendent, the vicar's mother. Early arrivals were already milling round the coffee bar but the centre of the melee was dominated by the generous, colourful figure of the operatic lady. She appeared to be recounting her latest spectacular successes with the Lower-somewhere-or-other Operatic Society's superb production of *Oklahoma!* and *The Sound of Music* to a large knot of people who were endeavouring determinedly to push past her to get at the coffee.

Meanwhile, the vicar, having shaken hands with everyone in sight at the back of the church, smiled sympathetically, disposed of the usual vitriolic complaints about the choice of hymns at the service, the dust of ages on the pews, the choir and the dead flowers round the font, now entered the coffee room holding a vigorous encouraging smile which she had already realized was so essential for her survival in this place. Even before she could reach the coffee bar she found herself discreetly side-tracked into a corner by four or five of the more prominent members of the matins congregation who congratulated her on her sermon ('That needed to be said, vicar') and threatened to boycott the service unless something was done immediately about the opera singer.

Of course, a stranger viewing the scene would have observed only a pleasant Sunday morning get-together and would have had no idea that a parish-shaking crisis was rapidly building to a climax. The parishioners determinedly avoiding the opera lady at the coffee bar and those in the corner threatening the vicar with a strike did all things with charming smiles and polite question. The matins congregation knew how to behave.

Some hours later, sitting at lunch in her bachelor flat overlooking the churchyard and talking to Boris her large black and white cat, the vicar reasoned out a solution for the opera-singer-at-matins crisis. She often found it helpful to talk to Boris about awkward situations because he always gave her his full attention and never argued. 'Yes, it could *just* work,' she told him as he sat tidily on the windowsill purring softly and regarding her alertly with his huge, unblinking eyes.

'Yes, let's do it,' she decided.

The vicar knew how to entice parishioners to meetings. At the end of the usual parish notices at Sunday service, you merely added – at matins only in this case – the date and time of 'a special meeting of some urgency' to be held in the church hall. You avoided giving any other details, thus ensuring that the unsatisfied curiosity would deliver a full, eager attendance on the night. 'The last thing I want is for the family service people to get wind of this,' she confided in Boris. 'The meeting must be for the matins congregation only.'

And the matins people turned up in force at the church hall. Only the opera singer was absent, being away on business that weekend, a circumstance of which the vicar made sure before putting her plan into action.

'Now this may sound odd to you,' she opened, as soon as everyone had settled in with their tea and biscuits, 'but I am sure you will all agree with me. As you know, our organist has been with us for 30 years this year and we all owe him a lot. As you also know, matins has always been his favourite service, so I thought it would be really wonderful if next Sunday we showed our appreciation by making a little presentation – with the whole con-gregation singing "Happy Birthday" at the start of the service.' She broke the ensuing dead silence with rising enthusiasm. 'He would be so *thrilled*,' she beamed. 'Because of your, er, tradition of not singing during matins, he really has no idea what you are capable of musically. He'll be *thrilled* that you are singing especially for him!'

No one quite knew how it happened, but by the time they left the meeting – very late – the matins congregation had raised the roof belting out uncontrollably 'Happy Birthday to you' two dozen times, and had gone on to wreak the same havoc on the specially chosen hymns for the birthday service. The uproar was truly awful and as the performers grew more and more enthusiastic discovering their voice capabilities even the vicar, who possessed a far from pleasant singing voice (they had called her 'corncrake' at college), could scarce restrain a shudder . . .

On Hacksaw's special Sunday the opera-singing lady arrived at church early and prepared herself to lead the matins music. She was vaguely surprised at the size of the congregation – the pews were packed – but considered that a larger than usual audience for her performance wasn't a bad idea. But then the vicar appeared and started talking about the organist, who had given so many years' service to the church and was loved by all. It seemed that some kind of presentation was given to him and then – then – 'Happy Birthday to you'. It was as if a nightmare from the nether regions arose around her with a sound that swallowed her up. It went on and on (the vicar had shouted, 'Come on! We can do better than that. Now then – again!').

There was a brief pause. She sat down weakly. Then came the first hymn. The nightmare returned. 'Glorious things of Thee are spoken'. Different keys and different tempos wrestled in a shattering crescendo. She swept up her bags, weaved to the door and fled.

The vicar spoke to Boris. 'Well, it worked. What a devious vicar I am. I wonder how the lady is faring at St James's. I believe their matins congregation don't sing either. She'll be all right there – as long as they haven't got a vicar like me.'

Boris thumped his tail.

3

The Window

The other day I came within an ace of ruining my artistic reputation and utterly disgracing myself. I was being shown around an ancient Dorset village church by the vicar, whom I had approached with my usual plea for permission to sing in the choir.

As we approached the east window I stopped, quite fascinated by it, and was about to say how much I admired the riot of colours and the flamboyant descriptive scrolls which garlanded the saintly, pink- and plum-coloured glass figures. Only in the nick of time did the vicar save me.

'Yes,' he said, sadly shaking his head. 'I know what you are thinking – a Victorian monstrosity of course, one of the few remaining signs of nineteenth-century vandalism in our glorious little church. I've managed to do away with the brass lectern and replace the font. And I'm trying to do something about the choir, which, forgive me for saying so, is really rather dreadful. But we'll still have to endure

the window for a considerable time, I'm afraid.'
And he smiled a tortured smile.

However, he had his plans. He was a very new man, full of ideas for the changing of everything that everyone liked in the church. For some months he had been endeavouring to work up a kind of Victorian-window-hating campaign, but even he had to admit that it wasn't progressing very spectacularly. In fact, the only person he could have vaguely called an ally was the art mistress at the local school. She was a fanatical disciple of modern art and was never happier than when teaching her pupils to draw two-headed ladies, and horses with five legs. But she was an atheist, and didn't approve of the vicar anyway. Among his own flock the vicar's campaign languished shockingly. He had brightly suggested removing the offending window and replacing it with modern tinted glass, as soon as someone would kindly die and leave the necessary cash. But the trouble was that no one ever seemed to die, and even those who were likely to didn't appear disposed to insert clauses in their wills about taking out Victorian stained-glass windows.

As for the church council, it seemed that they had no urge whatsoever to beautify the church. If they did anything at all, it would be something sensible like putting sorbo cushions in the pews, or fixing a green neon sign over the notice board. So the vicar carried on doggedly, forever hoping that one day someone would see the light and provide the financial backing to remove the annoying pink- and plum-coloured saints.

We moved on round the church and the vicar pointed out its various prized possessions – unique brasses and marbles and the tomb of a famous and most irreligious author. There was also a very inter- esting electric light switchboard. This was doubtless prized too, for it dated from the great pioneering days of electricity and gave off plentiful and severe shocks when operated. The vicar demonstrated this when he switched on the chancel lights and was nearly knocked off his feet. He explained mildly that there appeared to be some slight fault with the thing, but it was obvious that it didn't worry him as much as the Victorian window did. Lethal electric switches and even leaking gas pipes seldom worry artistic vicars when disgraceful Victorian windows are around.

We arrived now at the chancel, where a large, impressive lady wearing an apron covered with a hunting scene was sweeping peanut shells and toffee papers out of the choir stalls. She was so intent on her work that she never noticed us till she had swept most of the choristers' refuse into my trouser turn-ups. Then she said I was most welcome and would I be staying much longer, because she wanted to lock up the church.

The next day being Sunday, I was kindly taken to matins by one of the choirmen. He was the local baker, and boasted a very smart horse-and-van delivery turn-out which he also used for private transport. The horse was a knowing piebald animal called Charles II.

To make conversation I asked if there had been a Charles I, but he said certainly not. His horse had *always* been Charles II. And I fared no better when I broached the subject of the Victorian window. My companion informed me in a faintly surprised tone that the choir had nothing to do with the vicar, and knew very little about him. He appeared to have some queer ideas, but as long as he left the choir alone everything would be all right.

We parked Charles II and his van behind the chancel and tried to enter the vestry. We couldn't get far inside as the organist was holding a boys' practice, using a huge, battered grand piano that occupied about half the floor space and was wedged across the doorway. Some of the younger men were able to crawl on all fours round one end of the piano, but the others quite happily crowded in the doorway complaining about the local football team who had lost 12-0 on the previous day.

Eventually, at the last moment, the piano was

heaved aside and we all rushed for our robes as the vicar entered the vestry and gave vent to his usual Sunday morning grouse about the choir not being ready on time. When we were assembled in the stalls you could see that he was making gallant efforts to keep his eyes averted from both the dreadful window and the equally dreadful choir. Perhaps he sought consolation from the sight of his new font ('such a simple and beautiful thing'), or maybe he was glaring at a sidesman who wore squeaky boots and kept tramping up and down the aisles with stacks of hymn books. Anyway, his back was turned on us during most of the service.

In the sermon he told the congregation that they should strive to be *worthy* members of the church. If they were *unworthy* members, for example like a bad window or a slovenly choir, they did so *hinder* and give such a *wrong* impression. My friend the baker, who happened to hear this broadside, thereupon whispered to me that if the vicar was hinting that the choir should be messed about with, he was in for a big disappointment. The choir would still be the same long after the vicar had got himself made into a bishop and forgotten about their church. And as for the window, the only way he would get rid of that would be if someone put a brick through it.

At the close of the service, while the organist

was blasting everybody out of the church with a voluntary called 'Dawning Whispers', the vicar stood in the comparative peace of the churchyard thanking me for my services. Suddenly a loud crash of splintering glass halted his honeyed words. I saw his face light up with joyous hope. With eager steps he led me in the direction of the sound.

Behind the chancel a mob of choirboys had been playing football with a cricket ball. One of them had kicked it neatly through the window at the back of Charles II's bread van. I dared not look at the vicar, but Charles II looked straight at me. Then he raised his upper lip, threw back his head, and laughed as only a horse can laugh.

4

Reluctant Hero

The village church organist met me at the station
with his car. He had invited me to augment the
choir at evensong, after which, at a special supper,
a presentation was to be made to the oldest choir
member.

We now drove towards the outskirts of the village
to collect this gentleman. The veteran, Alfred, lived
with a married daughter in one of those between-
the-wars houses which estate agents amusingly call
desirable residences, but which the organist more
aptly described as a dump, where you enter by the
front door and find yourself in the back garden.
On the way I learned about Alfred.

He had sung in the choir for 70 years, had never
missed a service or practice, and proudly boasted
that he couldn't read a note of music. He had
learned all the tunes by heart as the organist ham-
mered them out every Friday evening, and as the
choir had tackled nothing new for the last half-
century, he was very proficient. He had never agreed

28

with either the vicar or the organist on anything. Of course, the vicar and the organist had never agreed with each other either, and Alfred had often been hard put to disagree with both at the same time. But he had always managed it, and had consequently led a very contented life.

As soon as we arrived at the vestry, two or three choirmen came forward to help Alfred robe. This proved to be rather tricky, because apart from the fact that he wouldn't take off his overcoat, and insisted on wearing a cassock several sizes too small for him, he said he objected strongly to people scratching around him like a lot of old women.

When he had eventually been trussed up like an ill-used parcel, the vicar politely enquired if he was sure he would not like to choose just *one* hymn, as this *was* his special day. Alfred replied that he certainly wouldn't, and appeared to grow really cross. Apparently he had earlier been offered the freedom of the hymn book and the anthem library for the whole service, but had pointed out that the vicar was paid to choose the music, and choose it he should.

Stainer, Dykes and Barnby had therefore been delved into deeply, in an effort to please, and I for one was delighted. But when Alfred saw the music list his indignation knew no bounds. After all these years, he fumed, that was gratitude for you – putting on stuff he didn't know – ignoring him . . .

A charming choirgirl, who said he was really quite an old dear, offered him a throat sweet. Taking a handful Alfred maintained that he didn't agree with such things – smelling the place out. He just had time to put half of them into his mouth before we processed into church.

The nave was packed to the last undusted pew behind the farthest pillar. It would be wrong to say that a sea of faces was turned towards us. This particular church was one of those where they display a large notice outside declaring, 'A warm welcome awaits you here', and when you get inside everyone glares at you as if you are someone from the income tax office. Tonight, therefore, even more than normally, the faces were all turned on each other, obviously keeping a sharp lookout for strangers who might be attempting to gatecrash evensong in order to qualify for the free presentation supper.

No one appeared to notice the choir until the vicar announced the first hymn. Alfred, whom Fate or some other unsportsmanlike character had placed next to me, now whispered in my ear that the whole thing would be ruined by the large bass opposite. He had only been in the choir 40 years, and according to Alfred was one of the rising generation who thought themselves too clever to heed what the organist told them.

Despite the bass, the hymn 'Ten thousand times ten thousand' was sung excellently, and I enjoyed it. I should have enjoyed it even more if Alfred hadn't dropped his large *A & M* on my foot at the end of the second verse, and told me I had a very funny voice at the end of the third. The spirit of celebration was in us all. It ran riot. We sang through that service with all the finesse and delicacy of supporters after a rugby international, or a charge of bull-elephants. Stainer, Dykes and Barnby never had it so good.

It seemed that in no time at all we were breathlessly making our way to the village hall for the presentation supper. But, fast as we moved, the congregation had got there first. They were already gathered in smiling groups round large plates of savouries, and were all agreeing that far too much fuss was being made of Alfred. With his voice he should have retired from the choir ages ago. Not that they wanted to be nasty about it, but after all he was *past* it. It was bad enough having a vicar who was past it. No one expected a vicar to know when he had had enough, but a choirman should have had more sense.

At the right moment the vicar butted in to make the presentation. He spoke of pillars of the church, and willing horses, and all the joy that Alfred had given with his beautiful bass – or was it tenor? –

voice, throughout the years. Long may he continue to do so, he concluded, and handed Alfred a large inscribed barometer.

Alfred studied it, amid frenzied cheering on all sides. When he could make himself heard, he replied briefly that he already had three barometers – presented when he had retired from the gasworks, the operatic society and the crematorium board, but he supposed he would be able to stick it on the wall in the scullery, if his daughter would move the mangle out of the way.

Alfred sat down. The guests cheered again and looked round discreetly for some more supper.

5

All for the Love of a Lady

George is a penfriend who lives in a tiny, tucked-away East Anglian village that still likes to keep itself to itself. Years ago he contacted me about one of my choir stories and as a result I now know almost as much about what goes on in his parish as I do in mine.

As far as George knows – and he has been in his village church choir for over 40 years with a bunch of other men who have also been in the choir for over 40 years – no woman in living memory has ever been a member of the choir. No woman has ever even applied to be a member. This situation goes back to the days when George and his colleagues were choirboys together. There was never any shortage of choirboys in the village church then. Churchgoing parents had two choices presented to them. Their small sons and daughters could join either the Sunday school or the choir. For the boys the favourite was always the choir. The Sunday

33

school was presided over by a highly respected, awe-inspiring lady secretly referred to as The Dragon and consisted of a bevy of superior-looking little girls all striving to be the favourite of The Dragon and strictly ignoring the rude, rough boys in the choir. Girls invariably found themselves in the Sunday school – indeed, their parents insisted on their daughters being correctly instructed in the Christian faith by The Dragon rather than picking up a highly suspect version of it in the choir.

The choirmaster was a small, wiry young man with a shock of uncontrollable red hair, but an otherwise well-groomed figure, a natty dresser in strictly conventional style who always sported a discreet buttonhole on Sundays. The choirboys addressed him strictly as 'Sir' and he never used their Christian names, always shouting at them by their surnames, with any additional names he thought appropriate at the moment. The boys, without exception, got on well with him and derived great enjoyment in calling each other by the never-ending variety of derogatory names he hurled at them when they displeased him with their efforts, or lack of them, during choir practice. They were all idiots, cretins, incredible oafs and morons, who year after year unfailingly won first-class awards at the local prestigious Christmas music festival and were in almost constant demand to perform at the more colourful village weddings. After each successful showing at the festival the choirmaster treated them all to a huge cream tea followed by front seats at the neighbouring town's annual pantomime. Here they really let themselves go in the traditional singing battle conducted by the dame and the demon king and while they were in full voice the choirmaster would hiss a message along the row to the effect that if they dared to produce such disgusting sounds at matins on Sunday he would throw every one of them out of the choir, lock, stock and barrel, even before they had finished the service, and that would mean no annual summer coach outing to Bognor, a riotous affair from which the vicar always firmly distanced himself...

As the years rolled on, the tradition of the village's all-male choir consolidated. The boys grew up and remained true to the choir, and the girls, no less constant and still looking askance at the choir, built up the familiar cohort of dedicated ladies who are the backbone of so many Anglican churches, those indomitable members of the congregation who quietly, consistently, decade after decade, manage (as George irreverently puts it) to keep the whole shaky show on the road. Ladies who, in the church's name, brew gallons of tea and bake tons of cakes, work wonders at the high altar with a few bunches of flowers and bits of bushes from the vicarage garden, ensure the pristine appearance of the vicar's vestments no matter how deplorable his outdoor attire, and with grim determination keep the choir's veteran robes from complete disintegration into mere swathing tatters. Those stalwart moppers and sweepers, ever ready at the close of the Sunday morning family service to tackle the unimaginable chaos left in the children's corner so that the incoming matins congregation won't be appalled and send vitriolic complaints and threats to the vicar.

Over the years the choir have not progressed so worthily as the ladies. After 40 years they still have the same choirmaster, still sing the same music, still wear the same cassocks that had reached the end of their useful life half a century ago ('but they are so comfortable to sling on and not worry about a dozen and a half buttons to do up'). The notorious summer coach outing to Bognor continues to flourish and the present-day choirboys still call the choirmaster 'Sir', although his original boys, now nearer 70 than seven, call him Charlie these days.

The present new, young bachelor vicar is inclined to be progressive, indeed very 'modern'. He is adored by the dedicated ladies because, as George says, he is very handsome, smiles a lot and 'lays on flattery with a trowel'. But he learned early in his ministry that you really get nowhere by upsetting the choir and organist and in order to introduce his thrilling plans for transforming the parish into the dynamic flagship of a relaunched diocese, he does his best to appear as appreciative and grateful to the choir as he is to the cohort of dedicated ladies to whom he really *is* appreciative and grateful. He is well aware that normally no one in the choir ever listens to a word of his vital, progressive, new-age sermons. Venerable custom deems that during sermon time the choir give all their attention to the more sensational Sunday papers and easy crosswords.

Hope springs eternal, however, and recently in the vestry after matins the vicar's fulsome praise for the choir's singing of some ten-page Victorian festival anthem, which roared on and on and forced him to reduce the length of his vital sermon in order to finish the service on time, was concluded with a broad hint that he was going to say some very nice things about the choir in his sermon next Sunday. This was so that they could hear themselves being praised and feel proud and gratified. There was method in his madness. His signalled reference to the choir did materialize, but tucked in at the very end of the sermon, thus obliging the choir to follow the vicar's entire performance before they could feel proud and gratified. The choir, however, soon detected the vicar's less than admirable motives and returned to the delights of reading more about the extraordinary goings-on of people in the Sunday tabloids.

And so life continued to meander along in George's village parish, much as it had done for the last 100 years, 'still untouched by time's rude hand', despite the forward-looking young vicar and the whole twenty-first-century changing Church of England.

Then, at the conclusion of choir practice on a certain Friday evening that the choir will never forget, Charlie, the choirmaster and organist whose wild red hair was now an even wilder silver and who still dressed nattily and sported a buttonhole on Sundays, this undoubted leader of the band of confirmed bachelors who were the heart and soul of the choir, announced firmly, even enthusiastically, that he was getting married. It seemed that the following stunned silence would have gone on for ever had it not been for one of the basses grabbing convulsively at his choir stall and accidentally knocking to the floor his hefty *A & M* hymnal. The choir was used to the bass knocking hymnals all over the place but this time the book had dislodged the choir's large brass collection plate, which now bowled clattering across the marble floor and spun clumsily on to the feet of the deliverer of the shattering news.

Apparently a well-camouflaged 'understanding' had been developing for some months between Charlie and one of the dedicated ladies, Rosie, who was a widow. And now the date for the wedding that would change the lives of the whole choir had been fixed and Charlie bravely faced his choir – all male, all amazed.

Later that Friday evening, as is our custom, George and I were speaking on the phone (we regularly put the world to rights in half an hour). 'I'm flabbergasted,' he stuttered unnecessarily. 'That Rosie was one of those snooty Sunday school girls when we were choirboys. They never had anything to do with us – not then and hardly much now. Well, that's what we thought anyway – and now we've got this Rosie and Charlie affair.'

'But Rosie's got Cleopatra, that monstrous black and white moggie who goes around terrorizing all the dogs for miles,' I said. 'Charlie has always hated cats, especially since the vicar's animal service last year when Cleopatra cornered Charlie's Karl under the vicar's pew and reduced him to a quivering jelly – and Karl is a champion Rottweiler too! Will Charlie have to take on Cleopatra as well as Rosie?'

George sighed down the phone loud and long. 'That's what love does,' he affirmed.

'What? Makes you brave?' I queried. 'Fearless?'

'Makes you lose your senses,' gloomed George.

'Y'see, it's not only Cleopatra. What's going to happen to the choir? Rosie and her dedicated mates will suddenly start taking notice of the choir now – and when that lot start taking notice they start taking over. Look at the way they got the men in the congregation to go to the coffee room with the women after the family service instead of sloping off to the Dog and Duck.'

'They don't care anything about tradition,' I said. 'They'll all start joining the choir – you'll be swamped – and I reckon the first thing they'll do is make sure the choir get those new cassocks, those the vicar's always trying to foist on you, the ones with all the buttons.'

'It doesn't bear thinking about,' groaned George.

Nevertheless, the choir had to bear thinking about it and despite Charlie's defection towards marriage they still backed him loyally, as their undisputed leader.

So, a week or two later, as if in a strange dream, they welcomed Rosie into their hallowed choir stalls and, as the bass who was prone to throwing *A & M*s about the place put it, they completed the surrender, as in an even stranger dream, by welcoming the rest of the dedicated ladies into the choir. Even those who couldn't read music and had no voices anyway succeeded splendidly in making a joyful noise throughout Charlie's and Rosie's wedding service and everyone remembered afterwards how splendid the choir looked and sounded and wondered why they hadn't thought of having new cassocks and ladies in the choir long ago. They made all the difference.

Rosie said that she was sure that her Cleopatra and Charlie's Karl would soon get on very well together – so long as Karl accepted that Cleopatra was in charge. Cleopatra had already taken over Karl's sleeping basket, so events were moving in the right direction.

6

Ways and Means

Groaner, the organist and choirmaster at the church where my cousin Eddie is in the choir, never says a kind word to his choir. After every service in which the choir takes part he joins them in the vestry and shouts things like, 'Well, I've heard a few pathetic efforts in my day, but this beats everything,' or, 'I was ashamed – *ashamed* – to be sitting there in charge of you lot,' or, 'Call yourselves a choir! – load of rubbish.' Then as he walks home he is invariably waylaid by enthusiastic members of the congregation who congratulate him on the music at the service, and he accepts their praises with genteel modesty and generously attributes any success to 'my very loyal and accomplished singers, whom I appreciate so much.'

During choir practice he never fails to tell the choir how very superior his singers of 20 and 30 years ago were, quite forgetting that these *are* his singers of 20 and 30 years ago. He has been in charge for years and years, and everyone stays with him for years and years.

Groaner's church forms one side of a delightful square in a small West country market town in a lively parish that boasts rather larger congregations than are usual these days. Sunday services include what is known as The Great Popular Family Service, to which everyone is always warmly welcomed, and choral matins, to which no one is ever welcomed, warmly or otherwise. However, there are a number of diehards, formal people who prefer not to dance in the aisles and hug each other or clap hands and stamp and knock balloons about the church while singing hymns, and these continue to come to matins, much to the sorrow of the forward-looking young vicar, who lives in hope that as the diehards die off he will be able to discontinue matins and channel all comers into the joy of The Great Popular Family Service.

Unfortunately there are those who enjoy the prayer book language and the kind of music used at matins, and if anything their numbers are growing, despite the vicar's ever larger multicoloured posters advertising The Great Popular Family Service which now completely cover the weatherbeaten notice-board, with its minute matins announcement.

Groaner's choir don't sing at the family service and the organ is ignored. The vicar prefers everyone to be as informal and partylike as possible and to bring guitars and drums, and sometimes there is lots of happy stereo music or someone plays the xylophone. But the choir don't waste their time while all this is going on; Groaner conducts choir practice in the vestry, telling the choir what he thinks of them until the church is tidied up after the jollifications of The Great Popular Family Service and is ready for matins.

Whenever I visit my cousin Eddie, it is taken for granted that I'll be singing in the choir at matins, and on this sunny July morning I was as always looking forward to the opportunity. We had just finished the practice and Groaner had lived up splendidly to his reputation of affectionately insulting everyone for a solid hour. Finally he grated, 'That's that, then. Goodness knows why those matins people stick it week after week, putting up with you lot. Mad, or martyrs, I reckon. Anyway, I suppose the circus has moved out of the church now, so we'd better get things organized.'

As Groaner clambered behind the choir stalls and opened up the console with a great rattling of keys and thumping of jammed doors, and two of the choirboys started distributing the music in the choir stalls, the last of The Great Popular Family Service revellers were meandering out of the church towards the coffee room, trailing small laughing or bawling children with deflating balloons and the remains of coloured streamers. One little girl sprawled in the doorway, red-pencilling a huge villainous-looking moustache on a poster picture of a popstar; and a wiry-looking little lady, struggling along behind an armful of home-made banners and shouting at everybody about not missing a very special parish get-together on Tuesday evening, fell over the little girl and shouted even louder.

Five minutes later the doorway had been cleared and the appearance of the verger, a regal, black-clad figure with immaculate imperial beard, and a well set up churchwarden in stylish pin-striped suit standing by a pile of prayer books and *Hymns Ancient & Modern*, set the correct scene for matins.

The church's fine peal of bells started to ring and the matins congregation began arriving, discreetly acknowledging each other and then settling down to see what the vicar had done to the latest parish magazine. It was not, of course, actually called the parish magazine nowadays. Since the arrival of the vicar two years ago, he had changed its name with almost every issue. The latest one, in fact, had no name. Instead, there appeared on the cover a photograph of the vicar pointing at the reader in the style of the famous World War One recruiting poster and saying, We Want You.

The choir were robed and waiting when the vicar bounced in, grasping half a mug of coffee and smiling vigorously. 'Splendid gathering at the family service this morning,' he enthused. 'Really terrific discussions going on in the coffee room. We're all so . . .'

'We're late,' grated Groaner. And forthwith we processed into the chancel and matins proceeded on its decorous way without a hint of balloons, banners, streamers, clappers or stampers. The first hymn, 'Through all the changing scenes of life', went well, although the vicar seemed to be gazing in puzzlement at the words in his book, which he made no attempt to sing. He seemed equally puzzled by the *Venite* and the psalm but, surprisingly, he cheered up tremendously when he came to read the first lesson, which was all about Samson getting his own back on some very unsavoury characters by pulling down a whole temple on them. My cousin, who sat next to me, explained that the vicar was really into dramatics like that. There was a lot of the actor in him; indeed it had been a toss-up whether he would go into the church or on to the stage.

When we came to the sermon, the vicar stuck to the rules and clambered into the pulpit, although he didn't like the idea of sermons. At The Great Popular Family Service he walked up and down the main aisle and conducted what he called 'an in-depth discussion among the family'. At matins he preached to the congregation.

As he got into his stride, telling the congregation that the church must look ahead and not be bound by tradition, must experiment with new forms of worship vital to today's needs, Eddie leaned close to me and said, in a whisper that could be heard at the other end of the church, 'He's not a bad sort really. He's got these funny ideas, that's all, but everyone likes him and he seems to like everyone – animals and all. Devoted to Alfie, he is.'

I knew who Alfie was. I could see him sitting fatly under the pulpit steps – a huge tabby cat with a knowing expression and a red velvet collar. 'Alfie likes matins better than the family service,' Eddie's huge whisper informed everyone. 'He used to come to the family service, but a few weeks ago they had some huge balloons to celebrate the vicar's birthday – not the ordinary ones, real monsters – and Alfie tackled one. It went off with such an explosion that it nearly frightened the life out of him. So now he comes to this service. You don't get that kind of thing at matins – not cats being blown up by balloons.'

The service ended with 'Guide me, O thou great redeemer'. This, as Eddie remarked, didn't seem to grab the vicar any more than the other matins hymns, and then Groaner played us out with the mighty strains of a Wagner grand march. The vicar hurried to the back of the church to see the congregation off. Unlike his style at The Great Popular Family Service, he didn't hug the women and slap the men on the back and call them 'Gert' and 'Joe'. At matins you always shook hands and addressed people with the correct style and, as far as the vicar could see, you always would.

The vicar came back into the vestry as the last of the choir were leaving. Dutifully he beamed and thanked them for all their hard work and then, releasing himself from his clerical collar, made his way to the coffee room in the hope that some of the family service members would still be there, continuing the in-depth conversation. They weren't. They were all sitting round little tables outside the coffee shop on the other side of the square, all talking at once. He hurried to join them, an unrestrained beam of pure joy breaking through the formal matins smile.

7

A Matter of Faith

One fine Saturday afternoon while on a summer cycling holiday in the West country I met the village vicar, a jovial Humpty-Dumpty character, as I wandered around admiring his homely Victorian church. Presently we got talking about church music and those who performed it and within minutes he had invited me to help out in the choir the next day. 'Half of them are away on holiday at the moment,' he explained, 'and the other half miss them so much they are all over the place even in the hymns they *know*. You'd be very welcome.'

I thanked him and assured him I would be delighted. 'Every little helps,' I said.

'Splendid! Great! Wonderful!' he exclaimed excitedly, as vicars are apt to exclaim excitedly these days on the rare occasions when someone is persuaded to join the shrinking choir.

'Is the choirmaster on holiday?' I asked.

'Oh, no,' the vicar said soberly. 'He never goes on holiday – he never lets up on the choir. It's almost as if he thinks they'll disappear if he's away. He's a perfectionist, you see. He can detect the slightest imperfection when the choir are singing and even in the middle of a service he will point to an offender and scowl in a most unsettling manner.' The vicar glanced around almost furtively in the empty church where we stood. 'He points at me sometimes. It puts me right off, you know.'

'There are some very disturbing choirmasters about,' I sympathized.

'But at least I don't feel singled out,' he continued. 'Knowing our choir, he's pointing at people all over the place right through the service. The choir are used to it, of course, and it doesn't worry them. They never take any notice anyway.'

In the choir vestry on Sunday morning I was made very welcome by the holiday-depleted choir, who told me all about themselves and asked all about me in a matter of minutes, and met another visiting choirman introduced as Hooter Harold, an alto who had been in the choir for years before moving to London. 'That was in the days when it was usual to have male altos in the choir – before all these contralto women took over,' growled a very obvious bass called Big Fred.

'Strange how contraltos always seem to be sort of battleaxe types,' mused a tenor whose wife and daughter sang soprano in the choir.

'That's only in stories and plays,' put in the organist, struggling into a veteran crumpled cassock with rolled-up sleeves. 'And in comic opera, of course – there's that wonderful woman in *The Mikado* . . . Katisha . . .'

'You don't have to go to comic opera to find 'em,' said the tenor. 'They started here years ago and caused no end of trouble. What about Fiona Cuttelthorpe, for instance!'

'I thought she turned into a bass,' said Hooter Harold.

'Only when she had a cold,' amended the tenor, 'or when Big Fred was away on one of his darts tournament tours . . .'

Then all discussion ceased abruptly as the choirmaster marched into the vestry and immediately commanded, 'Attention, choir!' He was an endlessly tall man of uncertain age with narrow, sharp features and sparse, prickly grey hair. He stood to attention by the piano. 'The anthem did not go well at practice on Friday,' he stated. 'It was, in fact, abysmal. It must be correct this morning, it must be nothing less than immaculate, perfect. For you to achieve this I must *insist* that you all watch me the *whole* time you are singing.'

And he went on and on. I whispered to the tenor, 'I don't know this anthem. I've never seen it before.

I *must* look at the music while we're singing. I can't watch him all the time.'

'It doesn't matter about that,' assured the tenor. 'Everybody will be looking at their music, or anywhere but at him, they always do. Y'see, when he conducts he develops these awful grimaces – quite demonic really – and turns a sort of rich purple in the face, awful to behold. He'll be pointing all over the place at everyone. Pointing helps him. He wouldn't know what to do with his hands otherwise.'

'I really don't know what to do about this,' I said.

'Just sing,' the tenor grinned encouragingly. 'It'll sound all right down in the congregation, that's what really matters. Down there they think anything's all right as long as the choir sings it and *they* don't have to. They appreciate us. They always give most generously to our summer outing fund – they really like us.'

'It doesn't sound as though your choirmaster likes you lot very much,' I ventured.

'Oh, no,' he agreed, 'he doesn't like us. He never stands any of us a drink even at Christmas, and if he meets us in the street when he's with his wife he looks annoyed and she kind of looks through us in a pained sort of way. She doesn't come to church but I think she's heard all about us. But we're vitally important to him, y'see – he looks on us as a challenge.'

'But he's been here for *years*,' said Hooter Harold, 'and the choir have *never* taken any notice of what he says.'

'True,' agreed the tenor, 'that's why we're such a big challenge. He revels in big challenges.'

I imagine we were indeed a really exciting challenge to him during the service. Whenever we were singing he was jabbing at all of us in lightning succession and, on more than one occasion, with both hands simultaneously. But the choir, with years of experience, I suppose, managed superbly to avoid eye contact with him and automatically took their timing from Big Fred, whose steamroller pace was so loudly imposed that we couldn't do much else. So we got through the hymns and psalms in a ponderous, dignified manner at half the speed indicated by the choirmaster's flaying fingers and distorted features.

Seemingly oblivious of the situation we plodded on until we reached the musical highlight of the service, the aforementioned anthem which I did not know. I enjoyed it nevertheless. It was one of those boisterous efforts turned out by the dozen by Victorian church musicians, the singing of which always makes my day. They also endear themselves to one for another reason. I'm ever fascinated by the evidence that so many Victorian composers chose to set to music some of the most incomprehensible, bloodthirsty passages in the Old Testament. The old favourite we now sang was no exception and we performed it with all the enthusiasm and power of a champion brass band blasting through a rattling good military march.

When we finished and sat down, rather breathlessly, and the choirmaster had mopped his face and returned it to a normal expression, the tenor, next to me, whispered that there would be a short silence now so that everyone could meditate on the words of the anthem. It was the vicar's idea, he explained, and the plan was that people could discuss their reactions over coffee after the service. He said that no one ever actually did this, however, because the words of the anthem were always so chopped up by the music that no one in the congregation could piece them together to make any kind of sense of them, while the choir only thought about the tune and seldom knew what the anthem was about. But the idea pleased the vicar because he had thought of it and it kept him in a good mood, so everyone was happy.

After the service, as I lingered in the coffee room with a small group of choristers who had not escaped immediately to the Goat and Compasses, the choirmaster approached me with measured step and solemn mien. 'Tell me,' he asked, 'what were you endeavouring to sing in the anthem? Was it alto or tenor – or were you attracted to the bass line?'

I laughed dutifully at his pointed remarks as you are supposed to laugh when dealing with choirmasters who make pointed remarks. I always remember the words of a very old, very experienced choirman who told me that if people wanted to enjoy being in a church choir it was essential that they never allowed themselves to become upset because the choirmaster hurled derogatory remarks at them regularly throughout entire choir rehearsals. He explained that choirmasters were artists and had artistic temperaments that could be seriously hurt when choir members got rebellious and failed to appreciate the outpourings of brilliant humour so generously offered at every choir practice.

The choirmaster seemed pleased at my reaction to his enquiry about my singing ability and looked as though he was about to linger with our group, whereupon the group gently and politely dissolved, leaving me with the choirmaster who was already deep into his cherished plans for making the choir the finest in England. He said they were the same plans, unaltered, that he had had since he was appointed 20 years ago. His faith in them had carried him through to the present day, even though the choir still hadn't changed a bit. But the vital point was that he had *faith* that he would eventually transform them. He really did believe that he could make a silk purse out of a pig's ear. All the pigs had to do was to watch him for every moment that he conducted and their performance would become pure perfection – as finest silk . . .

I thought a lot about that village choir and their choirmaster as I cycled away on my tour. Theirs was a happy lot. The choir enjoyed the way they sang unchanged over the years and – if they ever realized it – had simple faith that they would surely continue in their enjoyable tradition. The choirmaster was dauntless in his pioneering faith that in the fullness of time he would redeem them from their misguided ways.

All were happy in their faith. Faith was the answer.

8

No Vacancies

One of the first things that struck the new vicar when he took over at the East Anglian village church where my friend, affectionately known as the 'Orrible Organ Grinder ('Orrible for short), is organist and choirmaster was the smallness of the choir. Being himself quite unmusical and tone deaf, the vicar did not appear to be in the least affected by the nerve-shattering uproar that the small choir and organist inflicted on the congregation Sunday by Sunday as, in the words of the gloom-laden vicar's warden, they 'slaughtered the hymns and savaged the psalms'. It was the empty spaces in the seemingly endless Victorian choir stalls that worried and saddened the vicar, and moved him to plan a recruitment drive for more volunteers to 'have a go' in the choir. He said that in England, where congregations were always reluctant to sing above a whisper, unless they were on television, the great-est encouragement for them was to see the choir stalls packed with enthusiastic, joyful singers. Such enthusiasm and joy, he said, flowed out into the congregation in a great irresistible tide and in no time at all you had everyone simply raising the roof with praise.

The vicar's warden said that if the choir got even a little bit bigger everyone would raise the roof all right, but it wouldn't be with praise. Over the years the congregation had schooled themselves to put up with the choir in a most admirable, brave, Christian manner, but enough was enough and if the vicar started recruiting he would be pushing the choir's luck just that bit too far and would have a revolution on his hands.

Happily unaware of the warden's dire prophecy, the vicar blundered ahead with his 'Swell the glad sound' campaign with the greatest fervour. His wife, who was a bit of an artist between running single-handedly the seven-bedroomed eighteenth-century vicarage and making tons of chutney and jam for the Christmas bazaar, designed some delightful posters. They depicted heavenly-looking little choir people backed by bigger, noble-looking choir people all bawling their heads off, accompanied by a fiendishly lifelike representation of the 'Orrible Organ Grinder crouching over his console with all the stops out.

With touching enthusiasm the vicar was soon plastering the posters all over the village. And thereby, quite unconsciously, he inaugurated a very popular version of the type of competition that invites you to state, in not more than a dozen words, your views on something or other. Under the huge black printed exhortation to 'Join our Choir!' someone had written on the poster in the church porch: 'No experience necessary!'

And then the competition really got under way. Rapidly lengthening lists of similarly eye-catching remarks about the choir appeared on every available poster. In a number of cases writers returned again and again to add further flashes of literary brilliance. It was even rumoured that one or two highly re-spected, well-read members of the congregation had been observed inscribing their entries on posters late on dark nights, while others, who normally found it difficult to think what to say on a postcard from a holiday resort, eagerly scrawled their fulsome thoughts on the posters in the broad light of day.

'Orrible and his choir, who had been much dis-turbed when the vicar had first mooted the idea of recruiting more 'cheerful people to fill up the choir stalls', were intrigued by the way things were going. The choir was a sort of small select club whose members were closely related, always did things together, and had been there for years with the same hymn book, the same services, the same organist, and the same solid opposition to any new-fangled notions a vicar might suggest. They didn't take kindly to the idea of strangers barging into the choir and upsetting things, whether they were cheerful people or not, and, as 'Orrible pointed out to me when I arrived on a visit when the poster competition was at its height, what the vicars had got to realize was that they were merely ships that passed in the night. They stayed in a parish just long enough to change everything back to front and then moved on, whereas the choir were there all the time and couldn't be expected to take seriously the fads and fancies of someone who would be gone in a few years and followed by someone else who would alter everything again, so that no one knew what they were doing.

The new vicar, of course, soon became aware of the rude additions to the posters and wondered where he had gone wrong. Puzzlement deepened into dismay as the writings became more and more adventurous and eagerly vied with one another for the most atrocious insult (and, in some cases, atrocious spelling). He called a hasty meeting of the choir and organist to assure them that, as far as he and all right-minded members of the congregation were concerned, their efforts each Sunday were highly appreciated and much enjoyed, and he hoped they would take no notice of the unfortunate scrawlings on the posters.

'Orrible immediately sought to put the vicar's mind at ease. He said the choir couldn't care less about any number of unfortunate scrawlings and they certainly weren't going to change the habits of a lifetime. He added firmly that they didn't want any new people singing in the choir either. It had taken years to get the right balance and tone (brute force and ignorance, one poster had said), and even *one* new voice would stick out like a sore thumb and spoil the whole effect.

The vicar, despite his secret belief that by making everyone in the congregation feel wanted and important he could get them all to do just whatever he required to bring his pet plans for the parish to fruition, nevertheless sensed that he wasn't going to get round the choir with flattery. He began to rethink his tactics for eliminating the depressing gaps in the choir stalls.

Unexpected help was at hand. During a round of visiting some of the more prominent members of the congregation, he came upon a certain large, loud, very forthright lady who dragooned the church's flower-arranging team, and indeed most other members of the congregation whom she needed for frequent cleaning, renovating and tidying duties in the church and churchyard, and who constantly failed in their efforts to evade her at the back of the church after Sunday matins.

She and the new vicar appreciated and liked each other instantly. They favoured different methods of persuasion, but each realized that the other was doing a splendid job of managing what the lady called a 'cussed awkward congregation' – first-rate when you got through to them, but cussed awkward to deal with. And as for the choir, the lady, like the rest of the congregation, couldn't abide the thought of any enlargement, but in her case her consternation had nothing to do with singing. In fact she rather liked loud noises – she made plenty of noise herself. It generally meant that people were getting on with the job, she said. 'No!' she told the vicar. 'Filthy, dirty, ragged jeans, that's my objection.'

'Ah, er, oh dear,' murmured the vicar in some puzzlement.

'You see,' she explained, 'the choirboys never button up their cassocks – just sling 'em on and leave 'em gaping open. Consequently, as the choir stalls are open in the front, the ghastly sight that confronts me at every service is a row of filthy, dirty, ragged jeans.'

'I'll certainly speak to the choir and organist . . .' began the vicar.

'No good,' answered the lady. 'Can't do anything with that lot. No good pleading or threatening – I know! But I have a proposition, vicar.'

She explained that she had for some time been

considering making a gift to the church in memory of her late father. What if she gave a new set of choir stalls – with panelled fronts, of course – that would entirely hide the dreadful jeans? The vicar beamed and said that it would be a truly lovely gesture to give such a generous gift that would bear the name of her dear father. The lady said she didn't know about the dear father bit. He had been a dreadful old man who persistently smoked a foul pipe in bed, voted Labour and hadn't been inside a church since her christening – but she just couldn't endure the torture of the jeans much longer and new choir stalls would save her reason.

And right in the middle of evensong the next Sunday the vicar saw the light. The new choir stalls could also be a cure for his torture of the gaping empty places in the choir. The Victorians, catering for a huge choir, had taken up most of the chancel with stalls. The new ones needed to be only half their length. That way the choir would be bunched together in unbroken ranks – no depressing spaces. The vicar smiled and felt great satisfaction as he announced a hymn in the wrong place and the choir, regardless, bellowed forth with the anthem.

Some months later 'Orrible invited me to sing in the choir at the service of dedication of the new choir stalls. I am the one exception to their 'no outsiders' rule and I've often joined them when in the area because 'Orrible reckons my voice seems to fit in very well with their style and causes no harm at all. We had a splendid, uproarious service with the choir crammed into the new, shorter choir stalls, singing lots of martial Victorian hymns and 'Orrible's unique version of Handel's 'And the glory of the Lord', with not a pair of offending jeans in sight. The vicar too was well on form, ecstatically thanking the flower-arranging leader for her wonderful gift in memory of her, er, dear father. He then told the congregation how important they were to the life of the church and how very much he appreciated all their supportive efforts – and was there anyone who would kindly volunteer to take over the vicarage garden as the weeds were now waist high and he hadn't been used to a garden and wasn't a very good gardener?

Finally he announced that the extra space in the chancel resulting from the removal of the old choir stalls would be beautified with displays of flowers. More volunteers were therefore needed for the increased work of the flower-arranging team. The leader would be at the back of the church at the end of the service to take names.

There was a distinct feeling of relief that things were getting back to normal, that something awkward had been nicely avoided. The vicar was naively happy, the choir cautiously mollified, the uncommitted members of the congregation still hopeful that they could avoid the attention of the flower lady at the back of the church without actually appearing to do so – and the vicar's warden looked as miserable as ever. Life was tumbling along comfortably again.

9

The Choir Celebrates

A recently appointed lady vicar was rooting about among the church records and suddenly realized that her church building was approaching its two hundredth anniversary. She became very excited about this and, being an avid public relations devotee, had immediately approached the parochial church council with a request for ideas to mark the occasion. Truth to tell, the church involved is a quite undistinguished pile in the middle of a quite undistinguished village entirely surrounded by acres of potatoes. Few in the congregation seem to know or care how long the church has been there. They just go to church there because it is the only church for miles beyond the potatoes. One man, being approached for any information about the church's history, referred the enquirer to the choir because, he said, by the look of some of them they had been there from the day the church opened. But he is always rude about the choir, having some years ago been rejected as a member because of the tone-deaf quality of his voice and his habit of turning up late for every service, then complaining that someone was sitting in his place in the choir stalls.

My friend Maurice the Maestro, the organist and choirmaster there, shouts at the choir continuously throughout every Friday night choir practice and regularly upbraids them with the most lurid un-ecclesiastical language after service on Sundays. He has been with the choir for years and years and they all love him and derive the greatest enjoyment from forecasting among themselves which of them he will elect for his more outrageous insults each week.

The new vicar is always very diplomatic when dealing with him and evades all discussion likely to result in arguments about hymn tunes or Maurice's revered habit of lighting up a foul-smelling cigar in the vestry after matins. The question of the bicentenary was so important to the vicar, however, that she steeled herself to approach the maestro with words of seriousness well beyond the usual florid flattery about everybody being so indebted to Maurice for his splendid – yea, wholly dedicated – work with the choir. The vicar wondered if the choir could put on a very special concert for the great day. It would, she enthused, be so very much appreciated, so important, so enjoyed by all . . .

To quote the vicar's later words of relief to a

friend, 'The idea didn't ruffle the maestro's feathers in the least.' Indeed, he beamed at the vicar and almost eagerly agreed.

'I'll get them to do something comic – from Gilbert and Sullivan,' he decreed. 'They'll be much funnier than the authors intended. Nobody will even recognize anything as Gilbert and Sullivan but they'll bring the house down. They're musical morons, you see – they'll be a scream!'

The vicar was indeed thrilled at her unexpected success with the maestro and approached the next church council meeting with an excited feeling that she had already overcome the biggest obstacle to the realization of her bicentenary project. Normally she didn't approach meetings with the church council with any sort of exalted feelings. The members had so far flatly rejected any of her suggestions as too expensive or plain stupid, and usually went on to spend the rest of the meeting complaining about the icy coldness or tropical heat of the village hall where they were so bravely sitting and freely giving their time for the good of the parish.

But this meeting was different. The council members, suddenly aware that ideas for the celebrations were expected of them and equally suddenly aware that, being complete strangers to public relations theories, they couldn't think of anything – at least anything that wouldn't cost money –

immediately seized on the vicar's idea of a super-special choir concert as *just* the thing. Few of the council normally went within a mile of the choir except when they were obliged to on Sundays or at weddings but backing them now would get the council out of another fine mess the vicar had almost gotten them into. And, after all, it should be quite possible to put in a token appearance at the concert, spread a few nice warm words around and then fade out. Something of the vicar's triumphant feeling swept over them.

'Maurice and the Musical Morons,' whispered the chairman to himself. 'That would sound really with it!' The vote in favour of the concert was solid.

On the Sunday morning after the church council had unanimously lumbered the choir with the honour of providing the (only) event to celebrate their church's two centuries of service, Maurice surveyed the members of his choir in the vestry as they more or less prepared themselves to sing matins. 'In my wildest dreams,' he suddenly roared, 'in my most gruesome nightmares, I cannot begin to imagine why, but the fact remains, the church council have actually recommended that you lot should perform a concert – a *musical* concert – to mark this church's two hundredth anniversary. I try to imagine it, I try . . .'

A birdlike little contralto arranging her choir

gown with much precision before the vestry mirror turned towards Maurice smiling proudly. 'Quite right too,' she enthused. 'You see! The church council are at last acknowledging our undoubted abilities as singers, our pulling power, our unique contribution to church life in this place . . .'

Maurice, halted in full flow, gaped at her in bewilderment. 'You do realize,' he enquired, 'that after the choir, the church council – all of them – are the most musically ignorant people for miles?'

'But they know what they like,' put in the bass soloist, raising his eyes momentarily from the back sports page of his Sunday paper. 'Look at the terrific support we get when we sing carols around the pubs every Christmas. Why, last year when we sang at the Bull and Bear almost the entire evensong congregation were there to support us.'

'Almost the entire evensong congregation are in the Bull and Bear even when we are *not* there for them to support,' observed Maurice.

To ensure against 100 per cent non-attendance, Maurice fixed the first special choir practice for the Gilbert and Sullivan concert for a Monday evening well after all the TV soap opera episodes had been viewed and debated by the choir members. Maurice herded everyone on to the platform of the village hall and addressed them in the unique barracking manner they found so endearing. 'We are going to attempt some well-known choruses from G & S,' he announced. 'Musically adventurous and ambitious as I realize you all are, I nevertheless really cannot expose our audience, assuming we have one, to the excruciating experience of enduring any solos. Their Christian forgiveness when they are obliged to listen to solos at Sunday services is truly remarkable. I would not further impose on such magnanimity.'

'Will they mind enduring us exposing them to the choruses?' asked the bass soloist. 'Seeing as how it's for a good cause.'

'It will be heroic of them, indeed,' admitted Maurice. 'But then, our congregation are a heroic people. Our choruses are a mite less objectionable than our solos because everybody bawls away regardless and covers each other's blunders.'

'A glorious crescendo of melodious sound!' beamed the bass soloist.

'Anyway, our church wasn't built 200 years ago.'

The bass soloist had returned to his deep study of the back sports page, but Maurice heard clearly the words uttered so matter-of-factly by a little elderly man – the type you would never notice in a crowd, or even in no crowd at all. A little elderly man whose ever young, luxurious, romantic tenor voice had the ladies swooning in the pews and for which they were more than willing to brave anything the rest of the choir could hurl at them.

'What do you mean, wasn't built 200 years ago?' demanded Maurice urgently.

'Well, it wasn't,' insisted the romantic tenor. 'All those plans and papers and things the vicar found in the vestry broom cupboard were from All Saints up the other end of the fens.'

The bass put aside his sports pages, puzzled. 'That All Saints is luxury flats,' he said. 'My brother's got one. Very superior they are – fitted carpets throughout, full central heating, imitation electric coal fires, everything. Very superior conversion, All Saints was. My brother's flat is in the chancel and it's still got the big memorial window in the fitted kitchen. Very unusual that is – all that stained glass just over the cooker and the washing machine. Very nice.'

'Well, *that's* the place that's 200 years old,' explained the romantic tenor. 'When they cleared it out for the conversion they gave the plans and things to the vicar we had here then for safe-keeping, and that's how they came to be in our broom cupboard. This new lady vicar of ours is always poking about the place and upsetting things. Now she's dug out these papers and caused all this fuss.'

'Well, she's a historian,' excused the bass soloist.

'They often get things wrong. Anyway, I explained it all to her last night and now she's sulking.'

'I'm seeing her about all this,' announced Maurice very firmly. 'The comic concert is going ahead, of course. I've made all the arrangements, no matter what age our church is.'

'Built 1890,' supplied the romantic tenor, 'to replace the tin mission hall. My Great Uncle Hezekiah was the builder around these parts then. He did a good job at a bargain price – well, he *was* the vicar's warden.'

And so the Gilbert and Sullivan funny concert went ahead and was a resounding success. The whole village turned up and never laughed so much in all their lives.

The event had been advertised as an 'All Star Celebration Concert' and in view of the vicar's blunder over the age of the church, nobody quite knew what the concert was supposed to be celebrating. Unofficially most people saw it as a cautious rejoicing that the parish had managed to get along with the new lady vicar for the whole of her first year without more than the expected complaints and threats of resignation from the church council. In the eyes of everyone, however, the members of the choir have been stars ever since. 'Very effective,' commented Maurice the Maestro. 'Absolute idiots of course, but very effective.'

10

Hark! The Sound of Holy Voices

I was on my way to sing Sunday evensong in the choir of a village church a few miles outside the country market town where I was holidaying. I now stood in the new bus terminus – one of those places covered with concrete shelters from where you can travel to such delightful destinations as the Clodhoppers' Arms, Gallows Lane, Brutish Corner, and Broadway. (All country buses seem to go to Broadway, and you only know you've got there when the bus turns round in the middle of nowhere and starts to come back.)

On enquiry from an ancient gentleman, who was for some reason pushing a pram full of potatoes and empty beer bottles, and who obviously regarded my London accent with the deepest suspicion, I learned that I would have to take a bus to Lower-something-or-other and then walk round the village green and pick up another bus which would drop me at the church door.

I soon located my bus, which was already overflowing with people all talking without taking a breath. To my delight it moved off smartly within half an hour. The whole atmosphere was very friendly and informal and I noticed particularly that once clear of the town, the driver took no notice whatsoever of the official stops, but pulled up smilingly at the passengers' own front doors and back yards, or if they suddenly stepped out under his wheels from behind a tree, or wanted to pass him a box of eggs.

As the road became steadily narrower and more full of holes, so he increased his speed until everybody was bouncing and slithering off their seats. No one seemed to mind the bouncing and slithering, however, and the friendly roar of conversation continued unabated. Only the conductor (a dying breed in these driver-only days) stood aloof and rock-like at the back of the bus. As he thoughtfully turned the pages of the *News of the World* he whistled 'The Ride of the Valkyries' . . .

On reaching my stop I had no difficulty in finding the green where I was to make my connection. In the warm, still afternoon, it was completely deserted except for a bus driver who leaned against an empty bus, talking to a horse.

He seemed pleased to see me, and was most helpful. He said that as it was Sunday there was no bus running to my village, and I couldn't possibly get there, but perhaps I might like to go back to town in his bus, which left in an hour or so. But at that tense moment of decision another human being appeared who was obviously well acquainted with the driver. It transpired that he was the organist of the local church.

Seizing my opportunity, I introduced myself and my predicament, and offered my services. A few minutes later we were standing in the church, and the organist was making the usual apologies in advance for the hopeless state of the organ, and the shocking and uncontrollable behaviour of the choirboys.

Indicating a gentleman who appeared to be walking up the wall in a dark corner at the back of the building, the organist explained that he was doing something to the sound amplifying system which had recently been installed. It had been given by a very wealthy retired fishmonger who was almost stone deaf, but who always gave the largest donation to the choir outing fund in appreciation of their beautiful singing. His generosity over the sound system was mainly prompted by a desire to hear more clearly the vicar's sermons, with which he had never been known to agree. But, as his wife explained, the better he heard the more he could disagree, and that kept him happy right through the week.

In the vestry the choir were assembling, and I soon found myself cornered by that familiar, over-poweringly friendly character to be found in all self-respecting choirs, the Man Who Has Been There Longest. This one, a very tall, thin, stooping type, wearing what appeared to be the smallest choirboy's surplice, explained to me how things had altered since he had joined the choir in 1930. Naturally the present organist was the worst he had ever known – in fact the man was an idiot. Indeed, the vicar, a most unmusical man, had specially selected him because he knew even less about music than he (the vicar) did.

This, of course, gave the vicar a distinct advantage when he wished to upset everybody by changing a hymn tune or resurrecting an anthem which no one wanted to hear. The organist, who had a deep respect for the cloth, never 'saw through' the vicar, and consequently the vicar was very satisfied with him and everything worked smoothly.

As we entered the chancel the sound amplifying system was gently humming to itself. I caught sight of the operator, who had now descended from the wall and was smugly seated before a control panel containing enough knobs, dials, lights and levers to launch a space rocket. He was twiddling the knobs in a most expert manner, and had the vicar not hastily announced the first hymn I think we should have been treated to a really first-rate imitation of an American police car siren. In fact, according to the Man Who Has Been There Longest, the operator could produce every kind of sound from thunderstorms to cat fights, and now and again could even pick up the vicar's voice.

But the vicar was perhaps rather badly served in this respect. Apparently the operator had a curious habit of confusing his switches so that during the sermon the pulpit microphone was dead and the choir microphone alive. This meant that if you sat at the back of the church you couldn't distinguish a word the vicar was mumbling, but if you listened carefully, you could just hear the top choirboy running down the organist, and the top choirman politely requesting him to desist if he 'didn't want his block knocked off'.

When the service was over the organist explained that I couldn't get back to town by bus as the last one always left ten minutes before the end of the service, but that the sound system operator was going my way and would doubtless give me a lift. We walked to the back of the church where the last of the congregation were carefully ignoring the bookshelf, and leaving their hymn books all over the place. By this time the operator was again up the wall with the fishmonger's amplifier. He called down that he would be most happy to

78

oblige me as soon as he had made a few small adjustments.

He said that it wouldn't take more than an hour . . .

11

Contests at the Dog and Duck

My friend Terrible Ted is organist and choirmaster at the parish church in one of those impossibly picturesque, unspoilt English villages that seem to hold such irresistible attraction for writers of crafty rural crime novels. In reality, crime hasn't got much of a hold here and Ted is only called terrible because he is always driving an extremely noisy vintage sports car all round the village in the small hours, particularly in the vicinity of the vicarage where, late at night, the vicar is generally listening to soft, soothing music and gallantly endeavouring to convince himself that he loves all his flock, including the church council, the choir and even Terrible Ted.

In the coffee room after Sunday morning service the vicar wears his favourite sparkling smile, when he is not actually laughing uproariously at one of his standard funny stories which he recounts gleefully, effervescently, to anyone he can corner before they have had time to bolt their coffee and escape. He starts by asking how you are on this fine morning (no matter what the weather is doing outside) and before you can finish recounting your catalogue of woes he slaps you on the back and bellows, 'Jolly good! Splendid!' and rapidly moves on to his standard funny story – or just rapidly moves on. He repeats this action two or three dozen times until his triumphant progress is inevitably halted by Terrible Ted, the organist who blocks his way effectively with his outsize form and the usual words, 'Now, vicar, an urgent word about the choir.'

Mention of the choir always gives the vicar a nasty jolt, and never nastier than when the mention is by Terrible Ted himself. The organist has always got some sort of serious, vital, urgent question concerning the choir to 'hammer out' with the vicar and the vicar always listens with his special rapt attention expression and nods his head vigorously in agreement as Terrible Ted recites the choir's latest demands. ('Yes, I certainly agree. The cassocks have seen their best days – a new set in time for the Christmas services. Of course! I'll get the PCC moving on this right away – and many thanks for drawing my attention to this very important matter. We must look after our choir. I sometimes wonder what it would be like if we had no choir . . .')

And, generally speaking, there the matter ends. Both the vicar and the organist gently dismiss the subject from their minds and Terrible Ted concentrates on the choir's forthcoming complaint or demand scheduled for the next Sunday's coffee break. It's all a matter of revered tradition – and the choir, from generation to generation, have always been wholly dedicated to revered tradition. It is said that at the end of the nineteenth century the church council had an awful time trying to persuade the choir of those days to give up their individual ornamental brass oil lamps in the choir stalls in favour of new-fangled gas lights. There was an even greater row when they decided to do away with the traditional choirboy hand-pumping the organ in favour of an electric blower. Prominent on the organ case there is a photo of the last organ-blowing choirboy (now in his nineties and still bawling away in the choir as discordant as ever), who is still regarded with gratitude especially every time the electric blowing apparatus breaks down just before a big choral wedding service, or when Terrible Ted wants to celebrate his birthday or a win on the Lottery by playing his version of the 1812 overture after evensong.

And today, despite all the alarms and rumours of change, and realities of change, in the twenty-first century things at Terrible Ted's church are carrying on much as usual, with the vicar and the organist and choir, worthy opponents, dedicated to pulling in opposite directions with the admirable object of uniting the congregation in praise. All moves are very friendly, of course, and Ted's regular, total rejections of all the vicar's suggestions for trendy new praise songs, pepping up matins with a group with guitar and drums, and making evensong a quiet, meditative service without any music at all, are all firmly disposed of over a companionable pint in the Dog and Duck.

And the vicar goes on smiling and regarding the organist and choir as a great asset to the church. After all, within their number there are so many useful people – those who can work wonders in keeping the churchyard from becoming an overrun rubbish tip, those who happily work the unworkable vicarage boiler, those who replace dud lamps in impossible places many feet above the high altar without feeling dizzy and falling off the ladder, and those who organize the bar (as well as prop it up) at the annual summer fete and dance.

Deep down, the vicar does really appreciate the choir; indeed, it was this reality that contributed largely to the staging of the recent celebration of the hundredth anniversary of the opening of the organ. Preparations for the main event – a huge choral evensong – were given maximum publicity and the chief reporter on the local paper, who never went to church and had never heard the organ, described at length in a lead article its wonderful thrilling tone and called attention to Ted's superb keyboard skills and unique ability in training his splendid choir. A photo of Ted at the console with the veteran last organ-pumping 'choirboy' leaning heavily on his abandoned hand-pump handle completed the tribute. The chief reporter knew his job.

Tributes started to trickle, and soon to flood, into the newspaper office and the vicarage. As a sincere act of gratitude to Terrible Ted for being their leader and standing up for them against the vicar, the choir presented him with a pair of exclusive slim, patent leather shoes eminently suitable for dealing with the pedals of the organ. It seems that Ted had never thought of wearing any special footwear for playing the organ, and being a master builder (more than once his skills had prevented parts of the church from falling down) had always operated the pedals with his hefty steel-capped boots, which on occasion – in fact, very often – tended to operate more than the required pedals, rather muddying the resulting sound from the organ.

When the evening of the big celebration service arrived Ted had not succeeded in bringing himself to try on the new organ shoes. How can a man wedded to wearing massive armoured footwear – even about the house and at Rotary Club lunches and despite his wife's constant complaints about crushed carpets and broken tiles in the bathroom – even think of changing his traditional image?

Nevertheless, Ted arrived early at the choir vestry and made for the refuge of the small alcove behind the piano, there to attempt the near impossible feat of discarding his boots for things like ladies' gloves that were kind to organ pedals. As he wrestled to undo the leather thongs of a boot his agitated fingers worked them into a complicated, unco-operative knot that grew alarmingly tighter and tighter as the minutes passed. He held his breath! The knot was a clear message. It pointed to the way out of tonight's dilemma. He felt his conscience lighten. He had, had he not, genuinely tried to concentrate on the idea of wearing his new organ shoes, especially for this service, to let the choir see how much he appreciated their generous gift that threatened the custom of a lifetime, but now it was not to be. Fate had intervened. The time to start the service was at hand. There was no more time to deal with the knot.

He rose smiling happily and clumped into the organ box. The organ boy, the choirboy responsible for arranging his music at the console, met him in the doorway. He was Ted's valued treble soloist, who had the voice of an angel but no other leanings in that direction. He was now concentrating on peeling the wrapper from a very sticky-looking pep-permint. Without raising his eyes he informed Ted, 'The blooming pump switch won't work. Load of old rubbish, that blower is,' and scuttled away, neatly flicking the adhesive mint wrapper on to the ceiling.

The organ boy lost no time in informing the vicar of the blooming organ pump disaster. Unaccountably, startlingly, the vicar experienced an overwhelming glow of pure joy. While hastily summoning his full of sympathy and understanding expression he realized that a wonderful opportunity was unfolding before him. He would be understanding but firm with Terrible Ted and the choir. It was simply not sensible to bodge up the electric pump as they had done in numerous similar circumstances. The least the parish could do in appreciation of the many years of hard work Ted and the choir had put in and the pleasure they had given was to install a brand new electric pump for the organ. The job would, of course, take considerable time to accomplish, and although the veteran hand pump was still in semi-working order and could be used in the interim, it was very doubtful whether the original hand-pumping 'choirboy', who understood its ancient foibles, would be able to provide enough wind throughout a whole service at his age.

So during the time that the organ was out of action the vicar would suggest, yea insist, that choir and organist take a well-earned rest – and he would fill in the gaps with his guitar and drum group and introduce a whole range of relevant jolly praise songs. He was sure that the entire congregation would absolutely love the opportunity to sing themselves from the nineteenth century right into the twenty-first century. A wonderful new start!

Meanwhile, the organ thanksgiving service went ahead, the neglected hand pump being hastily reinstated. The pumping choirboy bent to his task with a will and the organ groaned into life, its wheezing, breathless notes blending with the rusty grating of the valiant hand pump. Throughout the service the sound blurted and disappeared in quick succession and when the final hymn was reached – 'Hark the Glad Sound' – the pipes gurgled into silence as the original pumping choirboy gave up the unequal struggle and mopped his brow with a large red handkerchief.

'It only wants a drop of oil here and there and a bloke a bit younger than me to handle it and it'll be fine,' was his verdict. 'I'll see to it, we just want a volunteer for me to teach.' Organ blowing by hand wasn't the easiest of things. You had to learn the knack.

On urgent investigation it turned out that all the

members of the choir were either too young or too old to man the pump, and this also applied to some extent to the congregation. Those members who did qualify all declined to offer, even after expert instruction from the original pumping choirboy, on the grounds that they were not going to make themselves look ridiculous, bouncing up and down behind the vicar's stall wrestling with an unco-operative piece of Victorian machinery, in front of a church full of friends and neighbours.

So now the vicar judged that the exact time had come for him to make his move. Over the prov-erbial pint in the Dog and Duck he beamed his most grateful, admiring smile at Terrible Ted and pressed home his offer of the well-deserved holiday for his cherished organist and choir. Terrible Ted appeared to be moved almost to tears by the vicar's great kindness and consideration. Why was this parish so favoured, so blessed, by having such a matchless leader? Of course, choir and organist would not dream of accepting the vicar's wonderful caring offer. They were privileged by being a major part of the vicar's parish team and they would not be absent at this awkward time with the organ blower. They would be there as always in the choir stalls and had already reached the unanimous con-clusion that once again the vicar would resolve an awkward problem. While they waited for the installation of the new electric blower it would be their vicar who would eventually save the day, as usual. It would be in his selfless nature to quietly step forward and man the old pump, the ever reliable leader. That's why the whole parish admired him. How blessed indeed was this parish.

So again Terrible Ted had prevailed at the Dog and Duck and the vicar continued to smile – and pump enthusiastically.

12

Unto the Third and Fourth Generation

In an endearingly unfashionable and battered part of London I came across a most interesting parish.

The church had been built to celebrate Queen Victoria's Diamond Jubilee, and the choir and the church council had been at loggerheads ever since. The church council's jealously guarded grievances were handed down unaltered from one generation to the next, and the present choir did precisely the same things to annoy as their grandfathers had done before them. A large proportion of the church council had always maintained that the choir should sing more popular music, and a similar proportion never ceased to demand that they should attempt more 'worthwhile' music. A small minority said that they shouldn't attempt anything at all, but they were the people who couldn't sing a note themselves and were rather frustrated.

Half an hour before Sunday evensong was due to start I made my way to the vestry, a delightful place full of wooden forms and lighted by low-powered electric light bulbs in converted gas globes. Its only occupants at that early hour were far too engrossed to notice me. A dreadful little boy with a head like a mop was painstakingly carving his name on the piano, and a refined-looking choirgirl was gently telling him that he shouldn't do it. She presently emphasized her words by knocking him from one end of the vestry to the other.

Picking himself up out of a cassock cupboard, the dreadful little boy told her in unprintable language that he would inform his big brother of her extraordinary behaviour, and that his big brother, who was a chucker-out at the wildest pub in town, would doubtless deal with the matter very drastically. This didn't seem to deter the choirgirl, who advanced on her prey with the obvious intention of repeating the treatment. Then she saw me and asked sweetly if there was anything she could do for me.

I answered respectfully that I would like to see the organist, and happily at that juncture the gentleman appeared. When he learned that I would like to sing in the choir he seemed quite pleased in a morbid sort of way. He said that it was an awful job trying to hold a choir together, particularly the boys. 'All morons,' he nodded sadly. 'Not like the boys of our day.' And remembering the budding criminals with whom I trained to sing, I wondered if his memory was playing tricks.

I had no time to meditate on this, however, because my attention was now attracted to a strange procession that appeared walking across the vestry. It consisted of five large gentlemen, dressed identically in black overcoats and bowler hats, who looked as if they were refugees from a Victorian wedding photo. They were followed by a girl wearing jeans and a pullover that reached below her knees. Without a word they climbed up a ladder and disappeared through the ceiling. 'There they go,' complained the organist bitterly, 'shattering the Sabbath peace!'

It transpired that these were the bell-ringers. What they did in the belfry each Sunday was considered very mysterious, and they had nothing to do with anybody. Nevertheless they evoked the organist's undying wrath. They always insisted on pealing the bells right up to the very last minute before the service, and therefore entirely spoilt his pre-service organ recital. For years he had deluded himself into believing that the congregation enjoyed his playing, and for years the bell-ringers had queered his pitch.

Members of the choir were beginning to arrive and an outbreak of mutiny among some of the boys hastily drew the organist away. I was now joined by a choirman who seemed very keen that I should form a favourable impression of the choir. He explained that I should not take too seriously anything I saw or heard in the vestry. It was all the manifestation of a great uneasiness among the choir.

And it was all the fault of the new vicar. He had swept into the parish like a new and very clumsy broom. With his fanatical smile and barrack-square bellow he had blundered happily from catastrophe to catastrophe. Within the first two months of his ministry he had upset almost everybody. Then, rushing in where angels and six preceding vicars had feared to tread, he had committed the monumental sin. He had proposed introducing a new hymn book. The choir were outraged. Indeed, on the Sunday following the announcement two of them had taken immediate steps to discover from the coverless wads of yellowing music in the choir stalls just what hymnal they *had* been using for the last 65 years, and the organist broke the habit of a lifetime by arriving at the church for matins without his *News of the World* to read during the sermon.

The choirman's fascinating story came to an abrupt halt at the entry of the vicar. Having inspected his troops and told us all we looked untidy, he straightened the boys' surplices and nearly tripped over his ragged cassock. Then he barked out the vestry prayer and gave the order to advance.

As soon as the service commenced it was obvious that his mind was still on the question of the new hymn book. A vicar knows that if he wants to make a change it's always a good idea to get the congregation to imagine that they thought of it first. And this vicar was really working at the idea. Each time he announced a hymn he apologized that the choir didn't have a *better* tune in their books or that the *correct* version of the words was not available to them. Then the sermon gave him his big chance.

But here the seed fell on extremely stony ground. To most of the congregation a hymn book was just a hymn book. They never sang the hymns anyway, and one book was as good as another to hold open at the wrong page. They wondered vaguely why the vicar was getting so hot under the collar . . .

Of course, the sermon thoroughly upset the choir and after the service they stood about in the churchyard in a state of revolt. Even the bell-ringers processing across the road to the Cat and Fiddle looked sympathetic. Only one choirman saw the bright side. He sat unperturbed on the church wall and propounded his theory. He had the greatest confidence in the church council, he said. They would take years to come to a decision about the vicar's hymn book and by that time, judging by the way the vicar was carrying on, someone high up would have noticed him and given him a job in a cathedral. Then the whole thing could be dropped.

13

Family Traditions

The new young vicar was happily convinced that
he was just the man the parish had been waiting
for. When his fresh, exciting, challenging ideas were
instantly and solidly rejected by the congregation
and the choir of the village church, he was not in
the least discouraged. He realized that they were
all busy people who, good souls that they were,
gave unstintingly of their precious time to the
church, but in the past had perhaps not been encouraged and taught how to use that time to best
effect in discussion, meditation and experimen-
tation that would result in a live, modern, dynamic
rural parish church, relating to today's vital needs
and aspirations.

But as my friend George, the church organist,
said, if this new man thought he was coming barging into the parish, altering all the service times,
changing the hymn book, telling people they were
an active part of the church and must do parish
visiting, even amalgamating the Monday night

men's club with the women's social hour because the church was one great united family, he had another think coming.

And the vicar, all energetic smiles and bubbling with gladsome enthusiasm, had dropped his biggest bombshell in the choir vestry just after evensong on only the third Sunday of his new ministry. 'Splendid singing,' he piped, effectively barring the way of the bulk of the choirmen who were purposefully moving out of the vestry towards their usual post-evensong relaxation at the Red Cow. 'I've got some really *great* new hymns that I must hear you sing, but, of course, the awful pity is that the congregation are denied so much of the enjoyment you give because there you are hidden away in the choir stalls behind that rather dreadful Victorian screen, when you should be sitting *with* the congregation encouraging them to sing as enthusiastically as you do. I know that you'll all agree with me that we are all one family, one community, not separated, isolated factions. How exciting it will be next Sunday, when the choir and congregation are all singing *together* – one united body *in the nave . . .*'

Among other things, the new vicar's vestry announcement completely upset my arrangement with George. Later that Sunday evening he was supposed to meet me at the station off the last train from London at the start of a two-week holiday I was to spend with him in the village. He wasn't there. No one was there except the porter who urgently trundled me off the platform and locked the gate behind us. Mounting his bike and running over my feet, he suggested that I was likely to find George in the Red Cow with the choir, where he always was if he wasn't in church blasting away on the organ. With a cheery nod he pedalled away into the autumn gloaming and I started on the three-mile trek to the village.

The uproar from the Red Cow assailed me long before I reached that ancient establishment. As I pushed my way into the surging mass in the bar, so many voices were shouting that I couldn't hear a word. A great wave of outrage enveloped me and flowed into the village street. I had met all the choir-men before, but no one replied to my 'Good evening', and it was only after George himself had related the latest of the new vicar's infamies to me three or four times over that he recognized who I was. The realization of the off-hand treatment I had been subjected to at the station made him even more outraged with the new vicar. 'I don't know,' he fumed, 'I really don't know . . . the irresponsible types we get foisted on us as vicars these days – full of stupid ideas and causing people to walk miles and miles . . .'

And the new vicar was, unfortunately, as good

as his word. When George and I arrived in the choir vestry for the following Sunday morning service – I had a permanent invitation to sing in the choir whenever I stayed in the village – the vicar was hovering around beamingly. He hovered and beamed until all the choir had arrived and robed and then, congratulating our four choirgirls on how pretty they looked and affecting not to hear the rather loud rude remarks George was making about people poking their noses into things they knew nothing about, he led us smartly down to the bottom of the church to the back three pews of the middle aisle.

'That's the *right* place for the choir to be,' he assured us, 'backing up the congregation with your splendid volume of sound.' He had apparently instructed the sidesmen to keep the three pews clear for us and to move forward any member of the congregation who fancied sitting there. A little trouble had arisen here, however, in the shape of a much revered and feared widow of a local general, who had sat in the same seat at the back of the church for 40 years (20 years with the general and 20 years without) and refused even to consider such nonsense as moving up a row.

The vicar held his smile and instructed us to fall in around her, with the result that I found myself sitting next to her in the place where no one had sat since the general had vacated it. I gave her a friendly smile, as I like to give all ladies, formidable or otherwise, but I don't think she quite trusted me because she immediately picked up her handbag from her side and placed it under her seat and gave me a very funny look.

Anyway, the vicar had now bounced back to his stall and announced that this morning everyone was going to have a good sing – a real family effort – and the first hymn would be the one on the piece of green paper that he hoped everyone had been given by the sidesmen. George struck up on the organ, but from the complete lack of any sound from the pews it was obvious that this was one of those hymns that appear more and more frequently these days via vicars who can't type, use pensioned-off duplicating apparatus and seem to like bits of coloured paper all over the place. If George had got it right on the organ, this hymn went to a tune which appeared to have been knocked together from 'Three blind mice' and 'Pop goes the weasel'. Even by the time we had reached the seventh verse, the words of which were cramped in an indecipher-able mass at the bottom of the bit of green paper, no one seemed to have got into the swing of the thing except the vicar, who ended up breathless and gasped, 'Wasn't that delightful?'

He seemed so elated that for a moment I had

the awful feeling that he was going to ask us to sing the whole thing again, but before he could regain his breath his attention was drawn to a loud, deliberate, slow tramping sound from the deserted choir stalls behind him. This was made by our sole contralto lady, who always arrived five minutes late for services, always wore riding boots, and had been in the choir for so long and had experienced the idio-syncrasies of so many vicars that, for years now, she had regarded them merely as ships that pass in the night and ignored all their edicts that didn't suit her.

We watched as she determinedly settled herself in her usual seat in the stalls, nodding graciously in response to George's welcoming wave from the organ and spurning the vicar's forceful traffic-police indications that she should proceed to the back of the church to join the rest of the choir.

Doubtless underlining a mental note of what to do with our renegade contralto, the vicar now pro-ceeded with the service and, in the course of the next half-hour, we sang with great gusto two well-known hymns from our usual hymn book. I don't think the vicar liked them, though, because he sat down throughout them and appeared to be medit-ating on his notes for what we used to know as the sermon but which, according to the latest parish magazine, was now to be regarded as a family chat.

Just before the family chat we were faced with another 'relevant, meaningful' new hymn, with a chorus of four words repeated three times, printed on the other side of the green paper. Then the vicar plunged into the chat, walking up and down the aisle and keeping his eye on everyone, instead of climbing into the pulpit from where he couldn't be sure whether those people at the back were hanging on his every word, or going to sleep behind a pillar, or taking a surreptitious glance at the sports page of their Sunday tabloids.

No one actually joined in the chat; it was one of those where the speaker takes for granted that every one of his listeners agrees with what he is saying. The vicar concluded each of his observations by sweeping us all with his well-held smile and proclaiming, 'And I'm sure we all agree on *that*,' or, 'And I know you will all fully endorse me on *this*.' The agreeing and endorsing went on for some 20 minutes, during which time the creaking and clattering from the choir's three back pews became noticeably louder and louder, members finding it a new and uncomfortable experience balancing themselves and their family Bible-sized *Ancient & Modern* hymn books on the slim planks of the pews instead of relaxing in the deep, discreet comfort of the choir stalls.

Finally we came to the offertory hymn at the end

of the service. It was 'Praise, my soul, the King of heaven', which the vicar said contained some fine words and soon we would have our own, brand new, more worthy tune to sing them to. This was being written specially by a friend of his who, he was sure we would all agree, was really great at hymn tunes. As we rose to sing, my reluctant neighbour, the general's widow, gave a loud sigh of exasperation and started straightening the piece of carpet on the seat where I had been sitting. For the rest of us the hymn, to Sir John Goss's tune, went well, as it always had done, although we did have a bit of bother in the choir pews. Normally, when the choir were in their official place behind the chancel screen, the collection plate was never passed round the choir stalls, but a sidesman who thought he was being funny now passed the plate round the three back pews. There was an awful lot of most unseemly fumbling under cassocks and surplices in an effort to find some money. It completely upset the choir and we missed singing the first two verses of the hymn altogether.

At the next meeting of the parochial church council it turned out that, from a vote taken at a large informal parish gathering at the Red Cow, it was very clear that, dear friends, soulmates and joyful fellow pilgrims as everyone was, the choir didn't want to sit with the congregation and the congregation didn't want to sit with the choir. The vicar tried most earnestly to convince members that they all really agreed with him, that his way was right for the new century, but the Red Cow decision was immovable. In the end, with a forgiving smile, he agreed to carry on in the usual arrangement 'and see how things go'.

Things have been back to normal and going well for some months now. The new vicar has rather forgotten the choir stalls issue. He's working on this idea of holding summer open-air services in the Red Cow car park, where there will be no divisions of stalls and screens, the choir will be mixed with the congregation and there will be no way of avoiding the collection or, for that matter, the vicar's family chat.

14

Tom, Tom and the Beauty

The choir music library in the country town church where my friend Stanley is organist and choirmaster doesn't conform to any known library standards. It consists of three large cardboard porridge oats cartons crammed with huge, disintegrating wads of music copies, all dating from the end of the nineteenth century. There are dozens of settings of the canticles and scores of anthems, of which Stanley's choir regularly performs two settings and three anthems. Stanley's choir is run on thoroughly democratic lines, and once a quarter members meet to choose the forthcoming music, which always turns out to be the same two settings and three anthems. Everything is very fair and satisfying, however, because although the same music is always chosen, it is chosen each time by different members of the choir so, as Stanley puts it, everyone has a fair crack of the whip. There's no need to do much rehearsing because everyone has known the stuff backwards for years and years. Everyone has also known everyone else for years and years. The senior members of the choir all went to school together and the junior members are all their children and grandchildren.

Stanley's choir is very traditional and very proud of its past. On the walls in the darker parts of the vestry, between great cupboardsful of fusty, pensioned-off cassocks and backless hymn books, are fading photographs of rows of demure-looking Victorian choirboys and extremely proper-looking choirmen flanking black-clad vicars and frightened-looking young curates, all lined up in the vicarage garden. There are also fading photographs of the same choirmen, on their own, looking not half so proper, wearing villainous bowler hats at rakish angles and clutching huge tankards of beer, at annual choir outings at Clacton.

Of course, as can be imagined in such a set-up, there are frequent presentations of chiming clocks, electroplated cake-stands and crates of alcoholic refreshment to members who have completed incredible numbers of years in the choir and long-service records are broken regularly. The latest champion is Top Line Tom, a venerable gentleman, so called because during his 65 years' unbroken membership he has never learned to read a note of music and always sings the soprano melody of the hymns in a heroic double-bass voice.

Stanley invited me to Tom's presentation ceremony, as I have often joined the choir during visits and know Tom and the two settings and three anthems very well. The vicar, who unlike so many vicars is a most enthusiastic supporter of the choir, certainly did us proud. To make sure that the atmosphere was really festive, he invited not only the choir and all known relations and looser connections, but also his usual rentacrowd, a party of really jolly people who could be depended on to make any function go with a swing and who were never seen in church or, for that matter, anywhere else in the town.

We all gathered in the church hall immediately after Sunday evensong on a fine, cold November evening. As usual there was the long line of trestle tables down the middle of the room, backed by the ladies of the refreshment committee who were in charge of the most heavenly fare. A collection of bottles with myriad labels, all quite unintelligible to me, were gathered round the splendid resident wooden barrel of beer inscribed in pokerwork 'Parish Church – Not to be Taken Away'. And as usual there was the hall caretaker, on his knees before a large, fearsome-looking gas heater that kept emitting loud popping noises and whistles but no heat whatsoever. The caretaker is very attached to this gas heater and always says that once it gets going the heat will be fantastic, but as far as I know it never has got going and has provided the caretaker with a warm sense of importance and being needed for countless years.

As soon as everyone had squeezed into convenient positions near the food and drink, the vicar, large and beaming and prematurely grasping a large, half-eaten sausage roll, clambered on to a chair and made his usual long-service speech, varying the time-honoured practice very slightly by presenting Tom with an automatic toaster. This was quite permissible, however, because Tom had already collected the usual chiming clock and the cake-stand at his 50- and 60-year celebrations. So for the next hour everybody ate and drank everything on offer on the trestle tables and nostalgically recalled Tom's early days in the choir, when things were exactly the same as they are today.

It was only when the company started to leave the hall, the junior members heading reluctantly for home and the main body eagerly for a second celebration at the Bird in Hand, that I realized I had left a book in the choir stalls. It was a book I'd never like to be without, called *Tom Brown at Oxford* – Thomas Hughes's not very successful sequel to his *Tom Brown's Schooldays*. Today no one seems to have heard of the sequel. It is out of print and gone. But I hold it in very great affection.

Magically, it can bring to life one of my favourite historical periods. Merely by dipping into it for a few minutes I am transported back to the Oxford of the 1840s and am at ease among all those characters I have known for years in surroundings that are as real to me as anywhere familiar to me today.

I first came across the novel in my late choirboy days when an earnest and trusting new curate hit upon the idea of slipping 'improving' books into the choir stalls in the hope that they would keep the boys reasonably interested and therefore comparatively noiseless during the half-hour sermons which were the fashion in those days. I don't think the ploy worked very well with my colleagues but *Tom Brown at Oxford* certainly worked with me. To this day I have never read the book outside church. Now well worn and frail, it still exclusively serves its original purpose of offering me an alternative to enduring a dull sermon, or one that I have heard, with minor variations, dozens of times before.

Stanley, who together with every member of the choir knows all about my attachment to the book, gave me the key of the vestry so that I could recover it immediately and said I'd know where to find him afterwards. I didn't need the key, however. The church was still open and a choirgirl was collecting the music copies in the choir stalls and sorting them into familiar-looking frayed bundles. She regarded me with a look of mock reproof that was quite captivating. 'You forgot your old friend Tom Brown,' she accused. She was in fact our male alto's granddaughter, an utterly charming girl who knew how to look shatteringly attractive even in one of the choir's regulation floursack ladies' gowns.

'These copies seem to be disappearing from the bottom up,' I remarked, examining a more than usually moth-eaten pile of anthems.

She regarded them affectionately. 'Yes,' she agreed. 'In that lot the bass line has almost completely worn away at the bottom of the pages. I'll have to copy it out and photocopy it and stick it over the rags.'

'That makes a lot of work. How good of you,' I ventured admiringly.

'Oh, it's nothing.' She smiled her delightful smile. 'I did the same thing with some other copies last month, only they were disappearing from the top and it was the soprano line that you couldn't read.'

'Marvellous,' I beamed, enchanted.

'It doesn't really matter, of course,' she explained, placing the wads in criss-cross fashion and carrying them to the music library in the porridge oats cartons. 'After all, we only *hold* the copies while we're singing. No one actually follows the music – Stanley says if we don't know it by now we never will – but it does look nicer from the point of view of the congregation if we're holding tidy copies and not things that look like bits of rag.'

She stepped back into the choir stalls and scooped up a collection of non-ecclesiastical literature that the choir members had left lying around on their seats – a *Dalton's Weekly*, a *Heavy Horse World*, two elderly issues of *Woman's Own*, a mail-order catalogue, a Barbara Cartland paperback and a list of local football fixtures. She placed them in two tidy piles at the end of each back stall. 'They need something to read during the sermon,' she observed.

I recalled the earnest young curate of my boyhood days who had inaugurated a similar scheme. Perhaps someone like him had once been at this church also. 'Have the choir always read during the sermon?' I asked, intrigued.

'Good gracious, yes,' she confirmed. 'Well, ever since the chancel screen was put up and the bottom of the choir was hidden from the congregation.' She laughed softly, with guileless hazel eyes. 'And the screen was put up to commemorate Queen Victoria's Diamond Jubilee.'

'You seem to know a lot about the choir history,' I said.

'You know,' she explained, 'my grandfather has been in the choir for ages and ages – he got his chiming clock over five years ago – and he can tell all sorts of stories. I was brought up on them. Mind you,' she added, frowning, 'regarding reading during the sermon, some of the choir get a bit annoyed these days when the vicar's away and we have this retired priest to take the services. You see, it's all to do with carthorses. The vicar's always been very keen on carthorses. He's even talked about getting rid of his old car and turning his garage into a stable so that he can keep a Shire horse as a pet.' The delightful smile returned. 'They are so lovely, don't you think? – great big, gorgeous, glossy things with huge fluffy hooves – but the buses are so awful round here and they've closed the railway, so he feels he must keep his car.'

'I'm with you,' I said.

'Oh!' She suddenly glanced up at the vestry clock, which permanently indicates five to six, and than down at her watch. 'You'll be missing the doings at the Bird in Hand.'

'I don't really drink,' I said.

She took off her choir robe and hung it up. It turned back into a floursack like all the others. 'Anyway,' she resumed, 'the vicar goes to all the horse shows he can find and lately he's been doing a bit of commentating in the heavy horse classes at some of the smaller shows. They're often held on Sundays and so sometimes he takes a day off.'

'And you're left with this retired man,' I concluded.

'Yes, and that's where the trouble comes in.' Her eyes sparkled and her smile was magic. 'He doesn't seem to know how to preach. No sooner is he up in the pulpit than he's down again. There's simply no time to read anything.'

'It's the way things are going,' I sympathized. 'Priests seem to have lost the art of preaching. Nowadays it's all meaningful dialogues over cups of coffee at the back of the church after the service.'

As we prepared to leave she locked up the organ console, after removing a half-bar of chocolate, some liquorice allsorts and a tomato from the lower keyboard. 'Stanley always has this trouble with eating,' she explained. 'No matter what he's eaten before the service, by the time we get to the anthem he's ravenous, so he keeps a little store in his music cupboard. It doesn't matter what it is as long as he can eat it.'

Suddenly she went back into the choir stalls. 'You're forgetting him again,' she called out, 'poor old Tom Brown.'

She reappeared, holding my battered old friend. I went to take it eagerly. She opened it and turned the pages. 'When I came back here to clean up tonight I started to read it,' she said. 'It looks rather interesting. You've carried it around for years. I'd like to discover its secret. Would you let me borrow it?'

I looked at Tom Brown. I looked at our male alto's beautiful granddaughter. 'Why, of course,' I capitulated. 'With pleasure. Yes! Delighted!'

15

Strange Goings-On

On my latest visit to my cousin Jack, who lives in a delightfully secret hideaway on the outskirts of a South of England country town. I was most impressed and encouraged to note that the choir of the local church where he is organist and choirmaster had nearly doubled in size since I had last joined them a few months previously. After choral matins on a golden, serene Sunday in June, we sat in the churchyard and Jack explained a few points to me.

'There are some very strange goings-on these days in one or two churches around here,' he informed me darkly. 'It was only when *their* choir people started turning up here and asking to join *our* choir that we found out.'

'Goings-on?' I prompted.

'Goings-on indeed,' he confirmed. 'It's all to do with new vicars.'

'Of course,' I agreed.

Apparently the new vicar of one of the churches

concerned was one of those who see it as their mission to break into the entertainment business by turning their churches into a sort of variety theatre-cum-concert hall and sports centre, with a small area tucked away in the vestry for the use of the persistently unprogressive minority who still expect to attend a church service on a Sunday instead of taking part in a vital Christian quiz or watching a meaningful, thought-provoking, multi-church review. Jack reckons that as soon as one of these show-biz clergy gets his way in a parish the first thing to be made redundant is the choir. It's just not considered at all progressive, vital or meaningful for congregations to stand about in pews listening to a choir chanting four-square psalms and singing hymns full of old-fashioned words.

The unfortunate choir in this case had not officially been made redundant, but members felt themselves to be such back numbers that they might as well not be there at all. 'So they looked around for a safe berth and thought of us,' explained Jack. And soon other refugees started turning up from another nearby church that also had a new vicar. Here, according to Jack, a great shake-up of the services had taken place, as a result of which prayers and 'praise songs' on bits of paper and cards and gaily-coloured leaflets had taken the place of the prayer and hymn books, and groups with guitars and drums had ousted the choir and organ. Pews had been ripped out and yellow plastic cafe-style chairs substituted, and the congregation were supposed to stamp and clap while they sang, and everybody had to keep on smiling and shaking hands.

Now the vicar of Jack's church is what Jack calls a proper clergyman. He conducts services in the traditional manner, dresses so that you can *see* he is a clergyman and, luckily for the choir, has no plans for moving on, retiring, or turning his church into a leisure centre, so the choir feel pretty safe at the moment. The new members are, however, a mixed blessing. The fact is that until the recent immigration of singers, all the members of Jack's choir belonged to one of three families who between them had provided the choir for about 200 years. Jack says that in situations like this you have to be very careful about letting in outsiders, but on the other hand one shouldn't look gift-horses in the mouth, and anyway the extra members will be very useful during the summer months when, in strict rotation, each of the three founder families goes on holiday en bloc, thus at a stroke reducing the choir by a third.

As a relative of Jack's, I'm accepted in the choir as family whenever I'm in the vicinity on a Sunday. I always enjoy myself and my latest visit was no exception. During choral evensong I sat next to one of the newly arrived refugees, a man who had been a sergeant major and a town crier, who kept on clearing his throat very determinedly and took no notice whatsoever of the marks of expression – or, for that matter, some of the actual notes – in his music but bellowed forth with gladsome voice and great enthusiasm. I could see he had got the idea all right and was settling down nicely in the traditional ways of our choir. He would be no trouble.

I wasn't so sure about others of the new recruits. One was a tall, thin man of uncertain age and voice who sang half a bar behind everyone else and during the anthem vigorously polished his glasses every time he missed a lead or came in at the wrong place. And directly in front of me in the soprano line was another new member, a middle-aged lady of spare appearance and darting steely eyes who, I feel, will have to mend her ways if she means to stay with us. While we were singing she kept up a loud sighing and tut-tutting and looked very cross indeed. And during the sermon she seemed to be pointing out things in the music in the most forceful manner to the choirgirl next to her, who had just offered her a surreptitious liquorice allsort. The choirgirl, a member of a founder family, appeared most puzzled by the new recruit's violent attitude, particularly as she (the choirgirl) couldn't read music and hadn't the faintest idea what the lady was hissing about.

After the service, the tall uncertain recruit continued to polish his glasses very enthusiastically and announced that he had enjoyed every minute of the singing. He reckoned that the choir had, perhaps, rather raced ahead of him a bit in one or two places – it was the kind of thing he had noticed in other choirs he'd sung with – but he was sure that they would sort out that little difficulty in time.

The cross lady soprano recruit, on the other hand, continued to be very cross indeed. As she placed her choir gown in a protective plastic cover and hung it as far as possible from all the other gowns and cassocks, suspended in a grubby jumble at the end of a tarnished brass rail, she was heard to remark to no one in particular that in the – although she said it herself – very professional City of London church choir, of which she had been a member before moving to the country, all singers had to pass stiff auditions and were not the sort of people who couldn't read music and were in the habit of passing round liquorice allsorts during the sermon. She would have to consider very carefully whether she could, after all, continue to lend her services to Jack's choir. One could not expect *too* much from amateurs, but there was a limit . . .

And it was during this time of uncertainty that

another complicated situation arose. The new local mayor, who had not been to church for years except for civic services and important weddings and funerals ('Love to come, I'm sure – many of my best friends are churchgoers – oh, yes – but you know how it is – the business and the council work – just no time'), had been giving thought to his forthcoming first civic service as mayor. He had suggested that instead of involving merely the parish church, as was the former custom, *all* the churches in the area should be involved in 'a really great get-together' of the congregations and choirs. 'After all,' he had told the local press, 'we all belong to one beautiful part of the country, one –' (he was about to say what he was always yearning for, 'one all-embracing party', but realized in the nick of time that this would definitely not go down well at the town hall with the opposition party) 'one happy, helping community,' he finished, using the phrase he had thought up quite unaided and had used with no little pride at countless party functions.

As soon as the mayor's view was made known, the parish church organist, an old friend of Jack's and, like him, a last-ditch traditionalist, phoned Jack.

'Can you imagine the kind of service they'll have to come up with to suit us *and* the do-it-yourself clappers and stampers?' he asked. Jack agreed that the mind boggled and reckoned that in particular the mayor and corporation in their robes and funny hats would have an awful job performing the activity bits.

'If it had been in the days when we all had the same prayer book and hymn books and you could walk into any church in the country and know what you'd be getting, the civic service would be easier to arrange,' said Jack.

'You knew the stuff word for word,' agreed the parish church organist, 'note for note, year after year. You could do it with your eyes shut. In fact, the mayor and corporation usually *did* have their eyes shut.'

'Particularly in the sermon,' said Jack.

'Those were the days. You knew where you were,' said the parish church organist.

'You *wonder* where you are now,' said Jack.

'I suppose they'll have some kind of rehearsal for the service,' speculated the parish church organist. 'Ah! Just think of it!'

Jack just thought of it – his choir and the parish church choir, the pop groups and the stampers and clappers, the professional soprano who didn't like liquorice allsorts being handed round, the man who had trouble with people always singing ahead of him, the mayor whose best friends were church-goers, the 'real' vicars, the 'show-biz' vicars, the

Book of Common Prayer, *Hymns A & M.* Not to mention the matins congregation at Jack's church who never went to any other service and would raise Cain if matins were cancelled for the civic service.

'See you at the rehearsal. Just think of it!' gloated the parish church organist.

16

The Way Things are Going

Brown Two and I come from the days when choir-boys were known strictly by their surnames – Christian names were never mentioned in church. In our choir there were three brothers Brown, and Brown Two was the middle one. All these years later we are still choristers, in church choirs many miles apart, and we still keep in touch about choir matters. Over the phone Brown Two was telling me that they had been having quite a bit of trouble in his village choir of late.

The trouble came from a number of sources. There was a new assistant curate, an over-the-top, chummy, enthusiastic young woman who could preach a stunning sermon and charm the hitherto impregnable parochial church council into eagerly agreeing to any revolutionary plans she hatched for dragging the church into its thrilling twenty-first century. Also, she couldn't sing and knew nothing about music, but kept pushing the choir to abandon their 'dreary, out-of-date hymns' in favour of a shoal of badly photocopied 'praise songs' on miscellaneous bits of paper, which gave no clue to the authors or composers concerned in their production.

Frederick (never Fred), the highly respected choirmaster who worked hard at his image of martinet traditionalist and eligible bachelor, said he could quite understand why no one wanted to admit responsibility for the songs and furthermore saw no reason why his choir's intelligence should be so insulted as to be obliged to sing them. Not, he readily agreed, that the choir were all that intelligent but there were limits . . .

Then there was the case of the promising young tenor, just married, who had committed himself in a weak moment to join his new wife's choir at the Baptist chapel. He had been lost. Two choirboys had been suspended for persistently causing an affray during the sermon at matins by letting loose their pet stag beetles among the smaller choirgirls; and the octogenarian bass soloist had at last fallen in love, got married and moved to the Costa del Sol.

'We're in a right state,' Brown Two confided to me, 'and if we have to put up with many more of the new curate's praise songs and people wrecking everything by getting married, and stag beetles all over the place I can see us ending up with no choir at all – no choir after 250 years!' He added gloomily, 'We've been here a long time, y'know!'

'And always highly respected,' I encouraged.

For a moment or two he thought about this. 'Well, not always *highly*,' he considered. 'There were one or two awkward occasions during the 1840s. In those days, of course, the singing was led from the gallery at the back of the church. None of the congregation ever ventured up there. It wasn't a nice place to be. It was full of discarded junk, belligerent mice and the choir with a fiddle and a trumpet.'

'So the choir were free to do what they liked,' I suggested.

'Not really,' he explained. 'There were always some busybodies around, just like now, and once or twice it was discovered that beer had been brought into the gallery by the choir.'

'But only for the men, surely,' I said.

'Oh, yes,' he agreed, 'but the whole choir copped it. Life can be most unjust to church choirs.'

'Still, whatever happened in the past, I'm sure your congregation *do* appreciate the choir today.' I sought to assure him. 'I'm sure they are concerned about your troubles at the moment.'

Brown Two became more disturbed. 'Oh they're behind us to a man,' he agreed, 'that's another of our troubles. I'm dead scared that four of them, whose anarchic vocal efforts slaughter the hymns regularly every Sunday, will be so concerned about us that they'll insist on joining the choir to help us out.'

'Well,' I said, trying to lift his spirits, 'at least they would help fill the gaps in the choir stalls.'

'Fill the gaps!' he gasped. 'As soon as they set foot in the choir stalls the rest of the choir would walk out. There'd be more gaps than ever. Then the slaughterers would loyally bring in more of the same ilk and we'd have a football hooligan chorus every time the vicar announced a hymn.'

'Your new curate would enjoy it,' I said. 'The hooligans could have a go at some of her new songs.' Brown Two groaned.

Things went from bad to worse for a time in Brown Two's village choir. A fond, fashion-conscious mother suddenly withdrew her twin six-year-old daughters because the choir's mauve cassocks simply didn't suit their colouring, or personalities, and made them cry. And halfway through evensong the next Sunday the organ broke down. It would have broken down years before had it not been for the organist's remarkable bodging-up skills, but now even those had failed.

The parochial church council were most upset about the twins' untimely exit from the choir but assured their mother that they quite understood the great difficulties posed by mauve cassocks, and would the young ladies graciously accept this six-pound box of chocolates? They roundly upbraided the organist for obviously neglecting a superb instrument on which the council hadn't spent a penny for 50 years.

Brown Two reflected on the growing tribulations of his choir on the first evening of one of my visits to his delightful village. He returned to the problem of the new assistant curate.

'Y'see,' he explained, 'she's a right nice young woman – very attractive really – but she's got this charisma thing in a big way. The vicar's absolutely thrilled with all her new ideas – sort of mesmerized, and backs her to the hilt in everything – sort of blind loyalty.'

'Sort of spellbound,' I added. 'Awkward.'

'More than that,' he warned. 'Dangerous. She just never stops her badgering about the choir singing her new praise songs. She's well in with a group who call themselves liberated poets and they churn out these praise things by the yard.'

'Liberated from what?' I asked.

'Oh, everything really,' he reckoned. 'All their stuff has to be relevant to today – and fun, of course. There must be nothing to do with tradition or convention, so they occasionally slip into their verses words like computer and spacecraft and you have to smile while you're singing them to show that you're enjoying the fun.'

A few months passed before Brown Two and I were again on the phone to each other. Without warning he had shattered my Sunday afternoon calm with a flash of the sort of news that is so intriguing it could only come from the vestry.

'Well, there you are,' he exclaimed. 'I never thought of a lady curate marrying – in fact I never thought of a lady curate.'

'Oh, they are around,' I assured him.

'Yes, and now ours is getting married,' he said. 'So, these things happen – but marrying *Frederick*, marrying our *choirmaster*! What will that mean to the choir?'

We each contemplated this unnerving question aghast and the phone line went dead for long moments. 'It all started with Frederick going to see the curate to complain about her pushing the choir to give up their hymn book and sing her songs,' recommended Brown Two.

'And what happened?' I asked.

'I don't know exactly,' he admitted.

'All we knew in the choir was that Frederick started disappearing like magic after every service and was hardly ever with us in the Pheasant after matins – and he's actually got us singing one of her praise songs at evensong.'

'That's how you get when you're in love,' I said. 'You're apt to do strange things.'

'Love! That's all very well,' he exploded, 'but what's going to happen to our hymn book? How are we going to keep out these praise things now? We shall soon be bawling them at every service. We'll be overwhelmed!'

Shortly after the marriage of the happy couple, I was again visiting Brown Two.

'It's been awful here,' he told me. 'Frederick is a changed man – almost unrecognizable. Do you know, at choir practice these days he never criticizes anyone. Never shouts, not even at Bert singing the bass solo in Goss's "Wilderness" – and he has *always* shouted at Ernie singing the bass solo in Goss's "Wilderness". And the other Sunday he didn't even seem to notice when we made a catastrophic mess of something by Vivaldi that we couldn't get the hang of. He never says anything but "Good" and "That's fine" and "So sorry I'm too busy to make it to the Pheasant with you after choir practice". He hasn't called us a pathetic bunch of morons or a disgrace to the church for weeks. He just keeps slipping in a new praise song whenever he can – even at matins – and smiling at everyone. Things are bad, I can tell you.'

Then events moved swiftly. The bright young assistant curate was suddenly promoted, to be a vicar in a team ministry miles away where her talents were doubtless sorely needed. Thus the village lost both their curate and their choirmaster, and hope dawned for the choir. Following the departure of Frederick and his bride the vicar, a kindly, comfortable, middle-aged bachelor, who was not at all musical and let the choir sing what they liked and joined them as and when he thought he knew the tune, made an announcement. He explained that in the present circumstances the parish would have to wait a while for a new curate, but a new choirmaster had already come forward.

One Sunday following evensong the choir were invited to the vicarage to meet the new man. He appeared reassuringly as almost a twin of the vicar. Over drinks and little sausage rolls the conversation turned to hymns. Yes, the new man was in *entire* agreement with the choir. Having praise songs with no authors and no composers smudged on odd bits of paper was *quite* awful. He wouldn't *dream* of such things. He rummaged in his briefcase and brought out a thick, pink and yellow, shiny-covered volume. Here was the solution. All the favourite new praise songs in one nice, clearly printed, easy-to-handle volume. How about that? Perfect, what!

I haven't heard from Brown Two for some time. I must phone him again. I'm sure he has another good story for me by now.

17

The Allotted Span

The choir of the village church where my friend Ernie sings all the tenor solos, because he is the only tenor they've got, are firm favourites of their vicar. He particularly appreciates the men of the choir. They all have vegetable and flower allotments just outside the parish where they meet regularly on Saturdays, amid the sheds and water butts, to talk sport and play cards. When the allotments begin to look rather too neglected they pull up a few weeds and tie up an occasional sagging bean frame or riotous clump of Michaelmas daisies. And although the vicar has no allotment it is a tradition that he is generally around too.

The organist also has an allotment, which presents itself as a kind of small natural lawn composed of self-sown grass, buttercups and dandelions in a cushion of undisturbed weeds. Here, in a red and white striped deckchair, he presides on warm summer Saturdays (in shed if wet) surrounded by the choirmen and here all important discussions about the choir – such as why they shouldn't try out a new 'praise song' suggested by the vicar's warden, and which pub to use for the next diocesan choir darts contest – take place.

When I made a recent visit to Ernie he took me with him to one of these allotment conferences. The choirmen sat about on the organist's lawn on various upturned boxes, a milking stool and a wheelbarrow with no wheel. My seat was an old car seat garlanded with uninhibited raspberry canes, and the vicar, beaming and relaxed, sat cross-legged in a comfortable clump of dock grass. The charge on the 'committee' on this occasion was the arranging of a special celebration party to mark the 60 years' service recently attained by The Oldest Member of the choir. Preparations for the function had been kept secret from him and it was intended to spring it on him the next Sunday. A large bass gentleman sought to balance himself more securely on the milking stool.

'Seeing as how we can't ask him what music he'd like for evensong on his Sunday, it's a bit difficult to know what he'd like,' he proffered profoundly.

'We *know* what he'd like,' said the organist. 'Anything that he knows the tune of so that he can really let rip.'

'He does that even when he *doesn't* know the tune,' put in a tall, thin alto folded in the mossy depths of the wheelbarrow.

'Anyway,' posed the organist, 'what about the presentation – what shall we give him?'

On cue everybody looked attentive and thoughtful. This was the question that always opened the age-old obligatory routine preceding a long-service award. The committee would put forward various suggestions and seriously mull them over for exactly ten minutes. It didn't matter what the suggestion was, as long as you showed interest by saying *something*, because you knew that it wouldn't be accepted. It was a revered tradition that when your time came for a long-service award you always got a chiming wall clock. Over the centuries dozens of such clocks had been awarded and no one saw the slightest reason why dozens more should not be awarded in the future.

But, as with everything else to do with the choir, a traditional routine had to be followed.

'Socks,' boomed the bass balancing on the milking stool. 'Lots of socks. He likes walking, doesn't he? Goes miles a day with his dogs and he wears holes in his socks all the time – he's always on about it. And there's that story that his wife has never mended any of them – throws them away.'

'He gets holes in his socks because his boots are too big,' said the wheelbarrow alto. 'I've *told* him about it.'

'What about a couple of pairs of the right-sized

boots then?' suggested another member. 'They would stop the holes and look like a better present.'

'We could give him a lawnmower,' said the organist, who always said, 'We could give him a lawnmower,' on these occasions. Everyone nodded and looked even more attentive and thoughtful. 'I could ask him for mine back then,' mused the organist. 'He's had it for two years.'

'I think a really nice, leather-bound copy of *Messiah* would be a good idea,' declared Ernie, reclining meditatively between the shafts of the alto's wheelbarrow.

'Or *The Damnation of Faust*,' supplemented the big bass. 'He's always going up to Town to the opera.'

'I think he goes to see Gilbert and Sullivan,' said the organist. 'I don't think he knows anything about *The Damnation of Faust*.'

There was a deep silence. The attentive, thoughtful expressions intensified. The alto unfolded himself from the wheelbarrow.

'I've got it!' he exclaimed. 'Why not treat him to a weekend in Paris – all expenses paid for two?'

Someone made a violent choking noise. Time for discussion was up. 'I know *exactly* what he'd like,' announced the organist. 'A chiming wall clock – that's the very thing.'

Everyone relaxed. 'Of course, perfect,' they chimed in. 'A chiming wall clock.'

The presentation party was splendidly organized by the vicar's warden who was, despite having his regular request for a favourite praise song totally ignored by the organist, a great champion of the choir. Nothing would have made him happier than to be in the choir himself, but being tone-deaf he realized that it would not be a very commendable idea. He did, however, have a young son of around four years old who, he felt sure, was destined for greatness in the musical world. Even at this early age, his father announced constantly to all who would listen, he was absolutely terrific on his set of drums, and recently Young Marvel, as his father now exclusively referred to him, had proved himself an absolute virtuoso on the mouth organ. He had been given a double-sided mouth organ for Christmas, and so determined was he to master the instrument that he blew it almost non-stop throughout the whole of Christmas Day and Boxing Day. His father said proudly that it made him think of the surprise and excitement that must have been felt by those privileged to first hear the child Mozart playing the organ. He was sure that his neighbours must have experienced much the same feelings when they heard Young Marvel on the mouth organ.

And now, he announced, Young Marvel would have his very first public engagement – at their presentation party.

On the Sunday evening of the presentation the church hall was soon crammed with the entire regular congregation, together with dozens of people who hadn't heard the choir sing since their wedding services, or when they had rallied round for grandfather's funeral. The scene inwardly shattered the vicar, an incurably shy man who found it tedious to deal with gatherings any bigger than the choir committee and who, despite his calling, was more at ease with books and flowers. He entered the hall unobtrusively via the kitchen. He searched desperately and unsuccessfully for a quiet corner where, hopefully, he could engage a choirman in prolonged conversation and avoid everyone else until such time as a decent escape could be made with a minimum of handshakes and encounters with people who wanted to know what he was getting at in his sermon at matins last Sunday.

The vicar was out of luck. As he edged into the hall, he was propelled firmly to the centre of the floor where, on a marble-topped pub table, stood the latest chiming clock, tied up with yards of yellow ribbon. And next to it, tightly blue-suited with glowing white shirt, gleaming black boots and the shining, smooth red face of an ancient cherub, stood The Oldest Member. His wife moved around him, frowning and removing invisible specks from his suit.

Normally, if they were meeting on the allotment, the vicar and The Oldest Member would have immediately fallen into animated conversation about cricket, or real ale, or ferrets and bees. But now, the sight of his friend wearing a suit, and with his wife, increased the vicar's unease. He reverted to his usual responses to new members of the congregation who tended to shake hands with him in the church porch after their first service and recount their life histories and how they had managed to end up in this particular village.

'Great. Splendid. Jolly good,' he exclaimed. 'Yes, indeed,' and turning a frantic smile on The Oldest Member's wife, backed well out of the way as the organist came forward to make the presentation. Suddenly realizing the main event was at hand, rather earlier than they had expected, the ladies behind the trestle tables full of empty glasses started sloshing white wine into and around them at a great rate until everyone held a dripping glass ready for the toast.

Reading from the identical script he had used for the last three choir presentations, the organist said how good it was to be here tonight to celebrate Albert's, er, beg pardon, George's attaining a magnificent 60 years' service in the choir. His splendid tenor voice had been a wonderful mainstay and he was sure it would remain so for many years to come. His colleagues felt that a chiming wall clock was most appropriate for one who, throughout all these years, had never been late for a service or practice. A record indeed.

Actually, the latter part of the script didn't really fit The Oldest Member. Being a very rough bass, he had never sung tenor splendidly and was always late for services and practices. No one appeared to notice this, however, and after the toast was drunk the cheering was long and frantic. His wife prodded him and ordered him to say something but luckily everyone had now turned their urgent attention to the tables loaded with the most appealing savouries and sweets. So The Oldest Member defiantly undid his jacket, loosened his tie and joined them.

And the evening went well. True, the vicar's warden had to waylay the vicar, just as he was escaping through the kitchen, to inform him that owing to the sudden indisposition of Young Marvel (who had surreptitiously sampled rather too many mixed savouries and sweets earlier in the evening) there would regretfully be no mouth organ recital. 'But don't worry,' the father had encouraged. 'He's agreed to play at evensong next Sunday.'

'Great. Splendid. Jolly good,' stuttered the vicar, increasing his stride rapidly. 'I'm sure the choir and organist will . . . Oh dear!'

18

Fight the Good Fight

Choirboys are culled from many sources. At my
uncle's severely practical parish church, which sticks
out like a sore thumb in an otherwise delightfully
vague Thames-side town, they get them from the
Sunday school. All boys joining the Sunday school
are given a short, sharp three weeks in which to
prove themselves. As soon as they have proved
themselves to be completely unmanageable and a
definite danger to the teacher, they are discreetly
drafted into the choir. They cannot then, of course,
continue in the Sunday school because the times of
the classes and matins coincide – this was an incredibly crafty move devised when the scheme was first
launched by the then vicar, who later became a very
successful Borstal chaplain.

But the boys' religious education is continued by
the provision of carefully chosen books (to be read
during the sermon only, and *not* during the singing
of the hymns) on manly saints, whose pictures
always represent them as very smart, modern young

men appearing rather uncomfortable in period costume, and extraordinarily old-fashioned-looking missionaries, who did great things in places with unpronounceable names in unmentionable heathen parts. These books in turn have an interesting habit of withdrawing themselves from the choir stalls within a very short while, in favour of certain multi-coloured American publications all about eight-feet-tall baseball player types with square heads and broken noses, who always seem to be fighting odd-looking gentlemen from other worlds, or rescuing attractive young ladies who look quite strong and well developed enough to fend for themselves.

Thus within a short period the boys' religious education is transformed from an out-of-date Victorian standard to a really vital, go-ahead modern one, which so recommends itself to our dynamic, new-thinking clerics.

The organist at my uncle's severely practical church is also severely practical. He never questions the methods employed to channel the local musical talent into his clutches. He never questions anything, and has always regarded the boys as unconvertible heathen or unbelievably stupid, or both. He therefore lives in his own pure and lofty world of music, and has instituted a scheme of gigantic fines for each wrongdoing, which ensures that at the end of each quarter nobody has any pay to come at all.

Contrary to expectations, the boys don't desert the choir. This is because the present vicar is a very athletic young man who arranges cricket and football matches each Saturday throughout the year. This arrangement, allied to the Sunday services, means that parents can get rid of their appalling offspring ('He's a good boy *really*, just a bit high-spirited at times') for the best part of the weekend, and is indeed so popular with parents that nobody dares leave the choir anyway.

It was half an hour before a Sunday evensong that my uncle took me along to church to meet the organist and make a brief appearance in the choir. The vestry was already full of choirboys causing a minor disturbance by throwing each other in and out of the cassock cupboards, turning the lights on and off, and proclaiming such sentiments as 'Up the Vikker' and 'Death to Dracular (Mus. B., F.R.C.O.)' in red pencil all over the choir notice-board.

Another disturbance was also going on. This was a major one, being executed with magnificent gusto by the bell-ringers, who seemed to consist entirely of very enthusiastic learners. My uncle said that apart from the tenor ringer they had all been learners for years and years and had never really mastered the art of keeping in time with the tenor man who was very professional, stone deaf and 94 years old.

I lip-read from my uncle that I should follow him, and presently found myself in a narrow passage with boarded walls that led, through a maze of buckets, mops, dead Christmas trees and pictures of stags and old vicars, to an iron corkscrew staircase up to the organ loft. And there, wrapped in gloom, morosely picking out the most discordant modern sounds he could produce, slumped the organist. I thought he looked an interesting man, and there was no doubt that he was an accomplished musician. No one who *wasn't* an accomplished musician could have coaxed an organ into making a noise like that, except perhaps my cat, who sometimes produces such sounds on the piano in the middle of the night when he wants to be let out.

My uncle had already forewarned me that the organist would be particularly wrapped in gloom at evensong because it was at that service that he had to compete with the bell-ringers, who were quite unable to appreciate beautiful sounds and always rang right across his performance. They always won the unequal contest because while he was a dedicated artist using a delicate, delightful instrument, they were nothing more than peasants, using brute force and ignorance.

The organist paused in his dedicated labours and shook hands with me. He said I would be very welcome in the choir. I returned the compliment by suggesting that I wouldn't wish to upset things by butting in, quite unrehearsed, and perhaps had better sit in the congregation. He wouldn't hear of this, however, and suddenly started making funny noises on the pedals. He said that no one, however bad, could further upset 'that lot downstairs'. I had seen the boys – wait till I saw the men! And anyway, I would feel a bit awkward in the congregation because they all sang in unison all the time and certainly wouldn't take kindly to anyone who was used to choir singing and harmonizing. It was something they were always very much against – most of them were on the church council and were always against everything, anyway.

For a moment the gloom on the organist's face almost lifted, as if some beautiful thought had gently crossed his mind.

'But we shall get the better of them tonight,' he mused. 'Seventy-three verses in the psalm tonight. Seventy-three! That's *really* tough to sing in unison. Even the fanatics fade out around verse 50!' He turned again to the console, and the organ produced another beautiful, nerve-shattering modern chord. For seconds it even drowned the sound of three of the bells which, by some complicated miscalculation, had just clashed simultaneously and gloriously with the tenor bell. The organist had forgotten me. A tiny triumphant smile flitted across his face and was gone . . .

When we returned to the vestry, the athletic young vicar had arrived and was picking up the choirboys out of the cassock cupboards and telling them that they should reserve all their energies for the football match against the daughter church choir team on Saturday. The choirboys of the daughter church always wore smart school uniforms, and sang very beautifully, and tried very hard, and never got fined for misbehaviour. They also always won the football matches against the parish church choir, who therefore considered them beneath contempt. So the athletic young vicar's exhortation had no effect on them whatsoever, and they continued happily throwing each other in and out of the cassock cupboards.

The vicar beamed at them proudly and gave my hand an athletic shake. By this time a number of the choirmen had also appeared, and he now introduced me to one who seemed to be their leader. He was a mountainous, ruddy-faced young man, wearing a yellow roll-necked pullover and a veteran pair of postman's trousers which, for some reason, were three or four sizes too small for him and were anchored halfway up his calves by chromium-plated cycle clips. He told me that he had been in the choir for over 20 years, boy and man. He said that most of the men had been in the choir for over 20 years.

'It's funny how it all happened really,' he mused. 'We all started in the Sunday school together, and the vicar at that time seemed very keen on music. We'd only been in the Sunday school for a week or two and he suddenly became very enthusiastic about us, and told us that we had the makings of first-rate choristers . . . We've been here ever since.' He seemed vaguely puzzled, I thought.

'There's one other point that rather fascinates me,' I confided to my uncle as we walked home after the service. 'Where *did* they get hold of those bell-ringers?'

My uncle gazed meditatively at two choirboys who were rejoicing in their release from a half-hour sermon on what a splendid game St Paul would have played if he had been a footballer, followed by a plainsong hymn with ten verses. They were deeply engrossed in rubbing each other's faces in a puddle caused by a clogged-up drain under the lych-gate, which the church council had been going to do something about for the last five years.

'Oh, the bell-ringers,' recalled my uncle. '*They* came from the Sunday school too. The tenor ringer used to be a Sunday school teacher in those days, but he ran out of stories and wouldn't go to the teachers' preparation class to learn any more – very stubborn, he can be. So the vicar said it would be a good idea for him to teach his class to ring the bells instead of ringing on his own every Sunday. They've all been ringers for over 20 years now . . .'

Like the leader of the choir, he seemed vaguely puzzled.

19

Muscular Christianity

When you are staying as a guest in the house of a friend, it is always rather difficult to decline to fall in with his suggestions of how you should spend your time. For some days I had explored the small Gloucestershire town and its surroundings, quite unimpeded, but on this particular morning my friend asked me if would like to help him do some moving. He wanted to lift some discarded choir stalls on to a coal lorry.

'They're solid oak,' he said, 'and they weigh *tons* and *tons*. They've been in the builder's yard ever since he took them out of the old chapel in the High Street – you know, the one that's been turned into a bingo hall.' He rubbed his hands together in pleasurable anticipation of a morning's brisk hard work. 'Those choir stalls haven't been touched for years,' he assured me. 'They're absolutely *filthy*. We'll have to clean them up before we move them. And of course we'll have to sweep up the coal lorry a bit.'

Now, quite frankly, I have never felt any great urge to lift filthy choir stalls weighing tons and tons on to either swept or unswept coal lorries, but in the circumstances I said I would be delighted. After all, as my friend pointed out, it was for a jolly good cause.

The jolly good cause was the annual carnival procession. This year the parish church was entering a float, and the idea of the choir stalls was entirely the vicar's brainwave. Some of the choir members who didn't like new ideas said it must have been more like a brainstorm; but then, they didn't understand much about publicity. Anyway, it was well known that the vicar would try anything once, and often more than once, especially if no one else wanted it. His present idea was to have the church choir actually standing in the choir stalls and singing Old English songs, interspersed with organ music played on a tape recorder concealed behind a dummy organ. Actual details about the completion of the float were a bit vague, but they had something to do with draping the coal lorry with flags and imitation grass, and pictures of the graveyard before and after the removal of the gravestones. There was also going to be a churchwarden sitting on the tail-board, giving away copies of the parish magazine that hadn't been sold on the previous Sunday.

When my friend and I reached the builder's yard, we found the vicar already in charge. He was pacing up and down, raring to go, a large, moon-faced, hearty man, with a voice that made it utterly impossible for the churchwardens in the back pew to doze off during the sermon. He kindly gave us a broom each, and set us to work on the discarded choir stalls. There didn't seem to be a broom for him, but he didn't complain. While we concentrated on our job, he examined the coal dust on the lorry and worked out the most efficient method of getting rid of it. As is usually the case, this was the most simple and straightforward method, and merely entailed my friend and I transferring our brooming efforts from the choir stalls to the lorry, while the vicar directed and encouraged us from a respectable distance.

After an hour or so of good hard work, everything was reasonably clean, and the vicar said we had done a good job, and roared with laughter at my blackened shirt. ('Nearly as black as some of the choir surplices! Ha! Ha!') He said we only had to give the stalls a good polish now and they would look like new again. But first we had get them up on the lorry. No good polishing them and then covering them with our black finger-marks!

Somehow I dragged myself on to the lorry and clutched at the end of a stall. I couldn't move it an inch. Of course, that is where my inexperience showed. As soon as the vicar explained to me how to hold the thing, and instructed my friend how to lift the other end, it was much easier. After only a dozen attempts, we had it balancing on the tail-board. The vicar applauded, 'Splendid! Jolly good!' and told my friend that it only wanted one good hefty shove to put it in place. I must admit he urged us on very well, and if we had been a tug-o'-war team I'm sure we would have won against the most tremendous odds, but somehow my friend hadn't quite mastered the art of doing the work of six men because he suddenly seemed to lose interest and made as if to fall down. But the vicar was there with his good hefty shove. It succeeded magnificently and drove me from one end of the lorry to the other, where I ended up, with the breath knocked out of me, between the end of the stall and the driving cab.

Success is a great stimulant. It only remained for us to lift the other end of the stall on to the lorry, and the job would be nearly done. The vicar said he was sure we would be all right now that we had the hang of the thing, and he was just going to pop round to the shop that was supplying the flags and imitation grass. He would also bring back a tin of polish, so that we could make a really first-class job of the stalls . . .

Deprived of the vicar's encouragement, we were rather slower in the placing of the second stall but, apart from a few minor injuries, we managed it very well, and our noisy gasping for breath was gradually subsiding as the vicar returned. He tossed us a seven-pound tin of polish and some nice new dusters. A really *vigorous* polishing was what was necessary, he said. And while we were doing that, he would pin up the decorations. It was, after all, the decorations that made or marred a float. He draped some mauve muslin right across the driving mirror and stood back to view it with evident delight and satisfaction.

Only one defect caused the vicar the smallest uncertainty about the superiority of the parish church float. The man who had made the dummy organ had made it a foot or so too wide for the coal lorry, and we couldn't use it. But, as usual, the vicar saved the day. He drove the lorry round to the vicarage, and very kindly allowed us to load his own piano on to it. As we dragged it on to the tail-board, he stood back and gazed at it with pride. He said they didn't make pianos like that these days. It was solid mahogany – had a good iron frame . . .

The carnival procession that evening was a great success. We watched it from my friend's front bed-room, where we lay propped up with cushions. The vicar, a brave imposing figure, stood on the parish church float, baton in hand, as he waited to conduct the choir in their Old English songs. But I understand that by the end of the procession he was looking just a little annoyed. The float had been followed directly by the town brass band, and they simply would *not* stop playing 'Colonel Bogey'.

20

The Voice that Breathed o'er Eden

There hadn't been a wedding in the village church choir for years. They had been passing through a period when the single members were either too young, too old, or too disinterested to take the brave step into the unknown. Then, suddenly, the first bass on the organ side got married. He created quite a sensation. No one imagined that the first bass on the organ side would ever get married, for apart from his choir-interest his one all-consuming passion was football. But he had met a girl who was quite willing to accompany him to football matches every Saturday afternoon of the season, and to agree with everything he said about the referee. So he got married.

The wedding was an eminently successful affair. Well-wishers and strangers, full of curiosity, made up the largest congregation within living memory, the choir overflowed the stalls, and the organist made his most glorious fiasco ever of the Wedding March.

And now, within months, a second member of the choir – the second bass on the organ side this time – was about to be married, and I had been invited by a friend, a relative of the bridegroom, to sing at the wedding and to attend a rehearsal of the special music. On our way to the vestry my friend kindly put me in the picture as far as the choir were concerned. Apparently their well-loved veteran organist had recently retired. Under his direction, they had sung nothing new for the last 40 years, and revelled in the prospect of continuing to sing nothing new for the next 40 years. There was, however, a slight ripple on their calm waters. The new organist held very advanced views on church music. He knew everything there was to know, and he knew that he was always right. If the vicar, or anyone else, asked him to perform music of which he didn't approve, he had a happy knack of dismissing it as 'grotesque'. He savoured the word. He used it often and with relish. The church seemed to be full of grotesque characters. He did not, however, include the choir in this category. He merely attributed their musical taste to monumental ignorance. In his lordly way he had a great affection for them and endured them cheerfully, rather as one endures a lovable but senile relative who is always insisting that nothing has gone right since Queen Victoria died.

For weeks now he had endeavoured to introduce them to the beauties of Tudor music, and to the extraordinarily clever tunelessness of modern church music. But although they remained most friendly, and regularly invited him for a drink at the Green Bull after Friday night choir practice, the choir made no musical progress whatsoever. Indeed, they secretly hoped that, if their vocal efforts mangled the Tudor and modern anthems thoroughly and consistently enough, the organist would give in and let them return to the Victorian works with which they were so happily familiar, and which he considered ought to be mangled anyway.

The forthcoming wedding service was the first to be taken by the new organist, and my friend expected a very good turn-out of choir members at the rehearsal. He explained that they were all very anxious to see that the organist didn't mess about with their colleague's choice of music. (He had sung in the choir for a long time, and knew what he liked.) You could never trust these new brainy musicians, who always wanted to alter things. If they didn't keep an eye on him, they would probably end up singing Tudor madrigals on the great day, and 'The Voice that Breathed o'er Eden' would be squeezed right out.

The choir vestry appeared to have been built to house a dog – a rather small dog who wouldn't want to move about very much. When we arrived, the miscellaneous collection of chairs and forms had been taken, and an overflow of about 20 choir members was standing in the cassock cupboards or sitting on a huge seventeenth-century oak chest which took up half the floor space and, I understood, contained three moth-eaten cassocks and a thriving community of mice.

The rehearsal had just commenced and had already run into trouble. One of the new organist's first acts had been to introduce a new and more enlightened hymn book, from which 'The Voice that Breathed o'er Eden' was firmly excluded. And as no one in the parish, churchgoer or not, had ever dreamed of having a wedding without it, this meant the resurrecting and dusting of the old and unenlightened hymn books from the stoke-hole.

I don't think much attention was paid to the dusting, because the book that was thrust into my hands still held some very definite traces of coke, which transferred themselves liberally all over my hands and clothes. The new organist, presiding at the piano, wore an expression of mingled shock and compassion as he obediently played through the first verse, and doubtless dreamed of lovelier things. Then he passed to the next item, which was the psalm, and here again he must have felt frustrated. The bridegroom had chosen a chant that the retired organist had specially composed for weddings, funerals, and the annual visit of the High Sheriff. It sounded like something out of *The Quaker Girl* and was very jolly.

The organist passed our performance without audible comment but, at the conclusion of one of the other hymns (this *was* in the new book, but the bridegroom had chosen a Welsh tune which was on a separate sheet and was affectionately referred to as 'chucking-out time in the Rhondda Valley'), he suggested that it would be a good idea if we didn't sing with *quite* so much vigour in the soft parts, otherwise nobody would know when we got to the loud parts. A man next to me muttered that he had never heard such rubbish. What did he think they were going to sing at – a funeral? The bridegroom would wonder what was going on if the choir started messing about whispering like that. The bridegroom was a very strong bass himself and always sang *most* heartily – even at funerals.

The wedding service was a great success. The choirman who had got married in the last days of the old organist maintained that you would never have guessed that a new man was at the organ. It was just like old times.

But there was a third choir wedding that year. The new organist also got married. And he was very insistent on the type of music he required. The choir were very loyal and turned up to a man. They sang the soft passages so softly that the congregation thought they had gone on strike, and there didn't seem to be any loud passages. The congregation are still wondering what it was all about.

The organist was highly delighted, because he *knew* it was a step in the right direction.

For months now he has been working on the choir with renewed hope and enthusiasm. But somehow he can't get them to take any more steps at all.

21

Horse Sense

It is a popular practice in the diocese in which my friend Alf is organist and choirmaster – at a most unfashionable, end-of-the-line red brick church – for various church choirs to be invited to sing Evensong at the cathedral while the regular choir is on summer vacation.

Alf's choir is never invited. This is generally thought to be because no one at the cathedral has ever heard of them, although the new sidesman, who is very embittered about the music at the church, reckons it's because someone at the cathedral *has* heard of them. The new sidesman is very embittered because he recently moved into the area and found it most difficult to locate a suitable church to which he might attach himself. Of the three in the neighbourhood, one was closed and being converted into luxury town flats (all with cable TV and imitation log fires), one had Sunday services that reminded him of scout jamborees and the third had Alf's choir. Eventually he had decided that Alf's choir was slightly the lesser of two evils, and the vicar was very nice and offered him a job as sidesman. So he joined the church to see what would happen. He hoped he could brave it out with the choir but realized how much he was asking of himself. At his former church the choir had sung beautiful, unaccompanied Medieval and Tudor music that had soothed and uplifted his spirit, whereas Alf's choir was always singing dreadful Victorian anthems at full blast that made his teeth ache.

During a recent visit to Alf, I took my place in the choir at Sunday Matins as usual and was delighted that for the anthem we were bellowing something by one of my favourite Victorian composers, Sir George Elvey, a long, rattling good piece, all sugary quartets and solos and heroic choruses. Elvey was organist at St George's Chapel, Windsor Castle, and organist to Her Majesty during a considerable period in the nineteenth century, and although 'those who know' may believe that his only lasting contribution to English church music is his tune 'St George', to the harvest hymn 'Come ye thankful people come', I have always derived the greatest pleasure from singing in any performance of his works that have come my way. I have a very soft spot for Sir George.

At the end of the anthem the choir knelt down exhilarated and well satisfied with their efforts, while the vicar led the prayers 'for all sorts and conditions of men, and especially on this St Cecilia's day, for all musicians – those singers and instrumentalists who give us so much pleasure through their talents'. He coughed and dropped his book. 'Also our choir and organist,' he added. In the choir vestry after the service when everyone was hastily hanging up their robes on a row of broken pegs and bent nails, or flinging them over the backs of equally broken and bent chairs, Alf called us together round the battered piano and said he had some unexpected news for us. We had been invited – indeed begged – by the vicar of a church some miles away to sing at a special service next Sunday afternoon. 'The trouble seems to be that someone there has got their dates mixed up,' explained Alf. 'Their choir is booked to sing three o'clock Evensong at the cathedral and at the same time there's this Horseman's Sunday service at the church. They're expecting scores of people and horses – and they'll expect a choir as well.'

For a moment the response was silence except for one of our basses who said 'Rubbish', but he had been in the choir for 50 years and always said 'Rubbish' when anyone mentioned doing anything out of the ordinary. And this situation was admittedly something very much out of the ordinary, particularly in view of the fact that the choir of the church seeking our help was one of those that sang the kind of music beloved of our new sidesman and was always winning prizes at important music festivals and giving recitals at inflated entrance prices in aid of the organ fund, whereas our choir never went near a music festival and no one had ever paid anything to hear us sing. 'Well, what about it?' asked Alf. 'Shall we have a go?'

'Does the Vicar know about this?' asked someone.

'Course,' assumed Alf, 'he was the one who got the phone call from *their* vicar. The vicar told me just before the service this morning.'

'What did he say?' asked the same questioner.

'Oh, the usual,' confirmed Alf. 'He thought the idea great, wonderful – and something to do with inter-church fellowship.'

'When he saw me just before the service,' supplied a flamboyantly decorative soprano who was arranging cascading blond hair before the cracked vestry mirror, 'he said, "How lovely". He always says "How lovely" when he sees me.'

'Heaven help us,' retorted a large contralto lady dressed entirely in dark brown with dark brown corrugated hair.

The rubbishing bass spoke again. 'Rubbish,' he said, 'and, besides, our choir wouldn't fit in with a congregation used to hearing all that Medieval wailing stuff. They wouldn't understand our good, hearty singing.'

162

'But we wouldn't have their usual congregation,' pointed out the decorative choir-girl excitedly. 'We'd have all those horsey people and I've got an idea that horsey people don't go in much for Medieval music – at least, the drayman down at the brewery stables don't. My uncle works there and what they sing in the bar on Saturday nights isn't Medieval at all.'

'Well, there you are!' beamed Alf. 'We wouldn't actually do drinking songs but we could do some Elvey. I reckon they'd like that . . .'

The horsey service was the most enjoyable the choir could remember for years. It was a kind of choral Evensong with the usual canticles replaced with hymns – well-known, roaring rollicking hymns all about heavenly armies coming down hard and heavy on evil hordes.

As the church emptied after the service the scene outside resembled a late Victorian painting, with horse carriages, brewers' drays, horse busses, costers' carts and people on horse-back dispersing in a clattering colourful jumble. And quite a crowd of well-wishers gathered at the choir vestry door as we came out, and our solo tenor, an ardent opera-goer was so moved that he declared it was like being outside the stage door of the Royal Opera House after a gala performance.

A gaunt, unendingly tall, immaculately attired

lady of uncertain age, leading a heavyweight hunter, barged through the crowd and grasped the first hand she came across – which happened to be mine. Applying a paralyzing grip, she announced, 'Splendid show – stirring stuff – right sort of hymns. And the, er, anthem thing – I've never heard anything like it in my life. What was it?' And Alf, always ready to help in the public relations department, butted in to say that our choir specialized in singing the type of music, and giving the type of performance, rarely heard in church today, so if she joined our church she could enjoy it every Sunday.

Back in our church a week or two after our 'great touring triumph', as Alf insisted on calling our emergency visit, the unexpected was still with us. As we assembled for choral Matins, our operatically inclined tenor came into the vestry excitedly and announced, 'There are a lot of those horsey people in church.'

'Rubbish,' said the bass.

'There are two pews of them,' insisted the tenor, 'and a horse tied to the railings around the back.'

'They've come to hear us again – they know a good thing when they come across it,' beamed the decorative soprano, edging the corrugated contralto from the cracked mirror.

The vicar, never missing a new face in church, had immediately welcomed the newcomers in his usual lovely, enthusiastic, swamping chummy manner that had successfully shattered the confidence of many a potential new member of the congregation, who had summoned up the courage to attend a service at an unfamiliar church. 'Great – splendid – well, well come on, do come up closer to the others. And there's coffee afterwards and you must meet us all – a really jolly bunch. Ah! we don't take no for an answer here. See you after the service.'

But these horsey ones were equal to the vicar. They'd come for a repeat performance of their horseman's Sunday service. They'd come to raise the roof with our choir, singing hymns that they remembered from early days at a service that came back to them with a comforting familiarity.

They are still coming. Some of them are on the church council now, some have joined the choir and gleefully add to the joyful racket kicked up each Sunday. And the parish is now preparing for its first ever horseman's service. There's tremendous interest and no one at all has complained at the idea of closing the church car park on the day so that they can get the horses in. Alf and the rubbishing bass (who hasn't been heard to say 'rubbish' for some time) are arranging for the local brewery to bring a four-horse dray, and the decorative soprano has a bewildering number of offers of a ride to church in a variety of attractive equipages . . .

22

Business as Usual

I noticed his name quite by accident while on a summer walking holiday in the West country. It was at the bottom of a notice stuck in the window of a tiny sweet shop in quietest rural Gloucestershire. 'COME EARLY', the notice urged in pen and ink capitals, 'for great bargains in the Monster Parish Jumble Sale. Unrepeatable offers. We open at 3 p.m. sharp.' And there was the name of the vicar – Marmaduke. The surname that followed struck no chord with me – I can never remember surnames anyway – but Marmaduke! How many priests, indeed how many men of any kind, are called Marmaduke these days? This simply had to be *the* Marmaduke, the one who, 20 years ago, was a curate at my local church.

Who could ever forget Marmaduke, with his huge bubbling enthusiasms and hopeless muck-ups of everything he tried to arrange? His bank holiday parish hikes were a feature that kept our church on the map. Always there was his huge figure with its uncontrollable shock of red hair, striding further and further ahead of us, looking like some rough-hewn wild god, his battered army knapsack swinging askew on his back, its loose straps flapping, and over his shoulder the rusty black umbrella that he never opened and was never without. We followed him at breakneck speed for miles and miles and hours and hours. When eventually we started losing walkers along the way and Marmaduke had disappeared ahead with only a few of the hardiest and most determined characters of the party still grimly hanging on to his tail, it usually fell to me to knock at the door of some outlying farmhouse to find out where we were.

Fiasco followed fiasco with Marmaduke. During the winter months he organized grand classical music concerts featuring distinguished singers and instrumentalists – he had a brother who was an orchestral conductor with many obliging musical friends – but on the big night, as often as not, our church choir had to deputize at short notice with a somewhat scaled down programme of music hall and drinking songs because Marmaduke had given the performers the wrong date or hadn't asked them at all.

People used to come for miles to see our parish pantomime, which Marmaduke wrote and produced each year. Lights would explode, scenery collapse and singers fall through trapdoors in the middle of romantic ballads. The good fairy would disappear abruptly on her wire halfway through her brave confrontation with the demon king and the sound system would suddenly make Prince Charming sound like a particularly tired and fed-up British Rail station announcer at the end of a long day of cancellations and signal failures. You could always rely on Marmaduke's pantomimes being far more entertaining than any script and there were different hilarious situations at each show. Patrons would come back night after night. No disaster, no unbelievable chaos ever deterred Marmaduke. He loved his work. He went on arranging even bigger and better muck-ups year after year. He was the most irrepressible, optimistic, cheerful person I had ever known.

And now I thought I had caught up with him again. Blundering fate had led me this summer Saturday evening to book for the night at the village's one and only inn. The lady in the sweet shop was most enthusiastic about supplying me with Marmaduke's telephone number and the loan of her telephone – ('A lovely man. The things he does – we never know what's going to happen next.') – with the result that I caught him in and confirmed that this was indeed the famous Marmaduke.

'How absolutely marvellous,' roared the phone,

reverberating around the cramped sweet bottles and biscuit tins. 'Yes! Do come into the choir at matins tomorrow. We're short – people ill and on holiday and having babies and things. You're a godsend. See you at the church in the morning. Marvellous! By Jove, yes!'

The next morning I reconnoitred the village and soon discovered the church, a venerable shambles surrounded by a huge graveyard full of hefty memorials leaning about at drunken angles under splendid fat oak trees. The main roof of the church was beautifully thatched and the choir vestry had a rusty, corrugated iron roof supporting clumps of undernourished weeds, pieces of broken noticeboard and a tractor tyre.

A teenage choirgirl with blatant good looks and a chorister's cap fixed at a most fetching angle on long blonde hair met me at the vestry door and said, 'Are you the one I'm looking for?' I introduced myself and confirmed that I had come to help out in the choir. 'Marmaduke told me about you. Come with me,' she invited, 'and I'll fix you up.'

She took my arm and led me into the choir vestry to a doorless cupboard containing a rail of choir robes. She stood back, eyeing me critically. 'Yes,' she decided, 'my brother's things'll fit you. He's away today. He's a steam buff. He belongs to one of those preserved railways. It's his turn to be fireman.'

The fireman brother's cassock and surplice fitted me perfectly and it seemed to me they were the smartest and cleanest garments in the cupboard, with none of the faded colours, rents and candle-grease splashes displayed by the others. She sensed my appreciation. 'My brother's a very natty dresser,' she said. 'You should see him when it's his turn to be a guard on his railway. He's got a uniform that makes him look like a field marshal.'

With some pride she started to trail me round the vestry introducing me to other members of the choir, who were now arriving.

She left me with an ancient gentleman who immediately told me he had been in the choir for 70 years and started regaling me with his recollections of life in the choir from his very first day as a probationer treble. It was rather difficult to see how I was ever going to move on from this gentleman, particularly as he had hemmed me into a corner and kept poking me further in with an authoritative finger as the saga unrolled. Then, just as we had got to the fateful outing on the eve of the World War Two, there was a clattering and confusion in the doorway and Marmaduke erupted into the vestry.

The wild red hair was still there, the great beaming face unlined. If anything, he had grown larger than ever. I recalled his handshake and was ready for its crushing intensity. Then the great fist clamped on to my shoulder and propelled me round the vestry to be introduced to the choristers all over again. Finally we arrived back to my choir-girl friend who had 'fixed me up'. Marmaduke's other huge hand drew her to us. 'She's our soprano soloist,' he said. 'Don't know what we'd do without her. She's got a brother in the choir too – real romantic tenor, but he's away today – gone somewhere to drive a steamroller.'

The soprano soloist had a most attractive smile. 'How do you do?' she said.

A tall, stooping man with a puzzled contemplative expression now entered the vestry. Taking not the slightest notice of anyone, he climbed out of sight into the organ loft. A sturdy red-faced choirboy who was trying to cram himself into a cassock two sizes too small for him nodded after him and informed me, 'He's my uncle. He plays the organ and he's wondering.'

'Ah,' I said.

'He's wondering what the vicar's going to do in the service,' he enlarged. 'We have to be ready for anything. The vicar gets sort of inspirations all of a sudden.'

'During the service?' I asked.

'Yes, right through mostly,' confirmed my informant, trying to tuck his cassock together where three buttons had burst off. 'Sometimes he changes a hymn just as we're starting to sing and sometimes we get a sermon to start with and another one at the end. Last Sunday he forgot to give out the last hymn, the one we sing to get the collection in. So everyone was clearing off without paying. But the vicar – Orange Marmalade, he's called – he went round the back and got a wheelbarrow and stood outside the door as they came out. He said he wanted a barrow full of money for the organ fund. The organ's got to be looked at – there's some people who sit in the front pew who say it's – er – excruciating or something, and it's not *all* my uncle's fault.'

'So no one falls asleep during the service here?' I said.

He winked. 'You'll see,' he answered gleefully.

Marmaduke having enthusiastically introduced me to the choir for the third time, we all filed in to the well-filled church for morning service which was, roughly speaking, prayer book matins with variations by Marmaduke. In place of the *Te Deum* we sang two war-like, heroic Victorian marching hymns, to which Marmaduke beat time with a huge booted foot, and he was halfway through the lesson about Elijah getting in touch with the prophets of Baal before he realized he had already read the two lessons set for the service. He carried on unperturbed, however, and said it was a jolly good action story anyway.

Finally, just before the blessing, he treated us to a talk on one of his favourite topics – the return of the tram to English cities. He said tram travel was a splendid way to foster the Christian community spirit – trams didn't pollute like buses or run along the gutter and splash mud over everyone in wet weather. He had fixed up a slide lecture on the return of the tram in the village hall for Thursday week. A voice from the organ loft bellowed hollowly, 'Wednesday!' – the organist was also a great tram enthusiast – and Marmaduke beamed and agreed and said, 'Of course, yes, Wednesday, er, fortnight . . . week.'

Outside in the churchyard after the service the whole congregation seemed to have gathered. No one was making for home. I found myself in the crowd next to my friend the soprano soloist. 'You're coming with us, aren't you?' she asked.

'Where?' I said.

'Marmaduke's walk, of course. Didn't he tell you? It's a regular thing – first Sunday in the month we always have a parish walk. It's great fun. No one knows what'll happen or where we'll end up.'

'I know what you mean,' I assured her.

Some three hours later I, with some other members of the choir and the organist, had finally given up the chase under a tree by a ditch in the middle of nowhere. 'I've never seen a tram,' the soprano soloist was saying, handing me half an orange.

'They're marvellous,' put in the organist, who was leaning against the tree in a semi-collapsed state. 'I remember them. Everything has to get out of the way for them and no hanging about. Trams *get* you there.'

I gazed down the seemingly endless sun-baked empty road across the ditch. In my mind's eye I saw the sleek, gleaming vehicle on silver rails, effortlessly, swiftly, gliding back to the village. I stirred my aching limbs. 'I think you're on the right track,' I sighed.

23

Period Piece

The vicar of my friend Archie's rural parish church is known locally as the appealing vicar. She has a most appealing smile that she employs shamelessly and to great effect fronting appeals for her many deserving causes.

She had a bright idea for bringing the church building to the notice of tourists, and local people who only came to church for weddings and funerals. At the meeting of the church council she enthused about 'the sixteenth-century gem that we are privileged to use as our parish church' and urged that its architectural glories should be made known far beyond the narrow confines of the regular congregation. The vicar proposed that a really super 'church open day' should be organized, backed by an effective advertising effort that would attract visitors from a wide area and (at a voluntary donation of £2 per person) make a lot of money for the flagging appeal for replacement of the church's historic, defunct boiler.

Archie reckoned the vicar got rather carried away about the 'sixteenth-century gem'. True, the bell tower had vestiges of sixteenth-century work in it but in order to save the whole place from falling down after centuries of neglect the Victorians had been obliged to restore it all over the place and now it appeared as a nice, homely jumble that would look pretty covered in snow on a Christmas card.

But the evidence of meddling Victorian restorers didn't worry the vicar in the slightest. 'The church is a sixteenth-century gem' – she liked the sound of that. That's what the advertisements would say. Once she had set her hand to the plough there was no turning back for the appealing vicar.

The members of the parochial church council, who knew from experience that if they wanted to get home from a council meeting before half-past midnight it was essential to endorse eagerly and immediately all the vicar's latest brainwaves, responded with delight to the open day plan to get a new boiler. They performed so well that they were walking free from a meeting before 10 o'clock – all lumbered with dozens of tasks to make the vicar's idea a reality.

And so, under the vicar's enthusiastic guidance preparations for the open day bounded ahead. The local paper got wind that something unusual was happening at the church even before they were officially notified, and sent along the keen young reporter of 'The Village Investigated' column ('What happened to the rubbish bin outside the fish and chip shop?' 'Why is the street lamp in front of the police station always on all day and out all night?') to find out if he could unearth a sensational, exclusive inside story. The appealing vicar was overjoyed to see him, and seating him firmly in an empty choir stall proceeded to recite a script she had just perfected for use on local radio. When he attempted to intervene with a question the vicar turned on him the warning smile that always silenced questions on the church council and cooed, 'Later, later.' Unfortunately, later the vicar was called away to deal with a couple who thought they wanted to get married and the keen young reporter, gratefully free to rise from the restricting choir stall, had to admit that with the best will in the world he couldn't create a sensational story out of the appealing vicar's script about raising money for a new church boiler.

His hopes rose again, however, when he dropped into the Fox and Duck for lunch and got into conversation with two of the church's oldest choirmen who, on receipt of free pints, were only too happy, yea eager, to regale him with their traditional, colourful and highly imaginative reports on what had gone on in the choir over the last 100 years.

The editor of the local paper commended the keen young reporter's resulting article as a job well done, but decided that the stories were so scandalous as to be unprintable. So, sadly, it was the appealing vicar's money-making script that appeared in the paper, tucked away in a bottom corner of the used-car adverts page, under a misspelt heading, 'Appalling vicar plans new project'.

Pushing forward with her open day vision of a constant stream of visitors from far and near, all gazing in reverent wonder at the architectural glories of her church, the vicar added to the vision the sight and sound of the choir giving regular, peerless performances of sixteenth-century music. The endless procession of admirers moved trance-like around the church and deposited their voluntary £2 donations for the boiler fund into the Victorian brass collection plate held out by the church treasurer, a large, forbidding man blocking the exit.

The vicar eagerly imparted details of her vision of the choir to the organist just after evensong. He had just pounded out the final chords of his favourite voluntary, a flamboyant, devil-may-care French piece that sounded like something played on a nineteenth-century steam roundabout organ.

The vicar smiled her famous appealing smile and said she was sure that the choir would respond in their usual wonderful, helpful fashion (the vicar's imagination knows no bounds at times) and come up with a programme of sixteenth-century music that would be the talk of the village and enhance their reputation no end. On quick reflection the organist thought that enhancing the kind of reputation the choir already had would do little to commend them to the hordes of sixteenth-century-loving visitors who were doubtless converging on the church. He had a problem. He turned to Archie.

Archie is his oldest friend, whose unrestrained bass voice underpins (some say undermines) the whole choir. He sings all the bass solos and thus saves the organist from having to ask the other bass to sing anything. The organist is very grateful for this because he doesn't like the other bass very much, owing to his habit of persistently parking his big builder's lorry right outside the organist's bijou Victorian terrace cottage with its reproduction stagecoach lamp by the front door.

Archie could see clearly the organist's dilemma. 'The choir haven't got any sixteenth-century music, have they? And they've never ever sung any sixteenth-century music, have they? Not a note.' He looked over his friend's shoulder at the wads of yellowing music copies that the organist had been vainly sifting through for the last two hours.

'I suppose it doesn't have to be actual *sacred*

music,' the organist considered. 'Here's a lot of stuff we used to sing at our concerts in aid of old people and old horses and things. They were *very* popular.' He undid the string of a bundle of music and disinterred a handful of copies: 'The Lost Chord', 'Come into the Garden, Maud', 'Any Old Iron'. He smiled reminiscently. 'They went down well years ago.'

'But not in the sixteenth century,' Archie reminded.

'No,' the organist agreed with a sigh. He examined a few more copies and sighed deeper. Suddenly he brightened. 'Tell you what!' he exclaimed excitedly. 'We could get the bell-ringers to kick up that din they always make every Sunday. All six bells have been here since the sixteenth century. It's all written on them – "John Whatsisname made mee 1580." I bet they'd keep all these visitors happy and the choir wouldn't have to sing at all.'

The bell-ringers, when approached, were tremendously keen about the idea of performing on the super church open day. It would give them the longed-for chance to ring for three solid hours, non-stop (instead of a few minutes before Sunday service), something they had been banned from doing since the memorable occasion some years ago when a raw beginners' mixed team of would-be and would-never-be ringers deafened and shattered the whole village for an entire Sunday afternoon. The bell-captain reckoned the team had improved a little since then and anyway, people could hardly complain so violently if the ring was in aid of a good cause like replacing a defunct church boiler.

The weather on the super church open day was perfect, a golden September Saturday – and the appealing vicar's 'Sixteenth-Century Gem' publicity attracted not a few coach parties who fancied a day in the country with a nice pub lunch and cream tea.

A handful of visitors who knew anything about sixteenth-century architecture were mildly annoyed when confronted by a church that was a shrine to Victorian ingenuity, but the vicar was so charming and full of fun that they soon found themselves enjoying everything, especially when they discovered that the Victorians had overlooked a fragment of the base of the bell tower that was pure sixteenth century. They sat around it on the grass, thrilled, until they could endure the demonic clashing of the bells no longer (the bell-ringers were indeed having their best time for years). Then they thanked the vicar profusely, contributed to the boiler fund most generously and joined the main body of the visitors who had variously pronounced the church 'ever so nice', 'ever so pretty' and 'ever so friendly, like', and were hurrying on their way to the real country pub lunch.

Urged on by the success of her super church open day scheme the appealing vicar resolved to repeat it. You could never have too much of a good thing. A few months later the papers carried a new advertisement: 'Super Church Open Day – come and discover our unique Victorian edifice.'

24

The Church Must Advertise

Recently I was a guest in the choir of a cheerful-looking, battered, hard-up, red brick, late Victorian church in a most unfashionable part of outer London where my friend Jake is organist and choirmaster. The new vicar – a sort of middle-aged dynamo with pronounced theatrical leanings – used choral matins to put forward his ideas for a church witness event in the form of a float in the town's forthcoming annual May Fair procession. For years the May Fair, organized by the local churches, had been held on the first Saturday in May on the permanently vandalized recreation ground. It had traditionally opened with, to quote the posters, 'a giant decorated carnival procession' that comprised an elderly council van hung about with paper streamers and six balloons, some members of the local dramatic society wearing outsize papier-mache heads and big boots, a pensioned-off diesel roadroller covered in vegetables, a man with a tin whistle, and the two or three town councillors (in full dress) who could be persuaded to get out of bed before ten o'clock on a Saturday morning.

Like the majority of the town councillors, the bulk of the population didn't see any reason to rise before ten o'clock on a Saturday, even on May Fair day, so the volume of support along the processional route was normally thin to non-existent. In any case, the procession got so strung out and merged in with the through traffic along the main road that any spectators had always completely disappeared long before the procession reached the fairground.

The big crowds did materialize, however, some two hours later when the central point of the proceedings, the colossal beer tent, was opened and its satellite 'antique' and 'fashion' stalls had been loaded with tons of rubbish specially culled from attics, garages and garden sheds for miles around. The weather always seemed to be fine and the crowds always increased to frightening proportions. They drank all the beer and purchased all the rubbish, and everyone went home and pronounced the fair another great success.

But the opening procession remained a sad, lonely, almost unknown outcast. And the new vicar had decided to do something about it. So on this Sunday morning he strode up and down the aisle faster and faster as his inspirations for the church

184

float tumbled over each other. 'You see, the church has got to advertise,' he enthused. 'We must be seen to be believed.' He has a way of emphasizing a point by suddenly pointing to someone and holding the stance in perfect silence for a number of seconds before shouting, 'Imagine! Just imagine . . .'

This time he swung round and targeted our bass soloist who was dozing gently in the choir stalls. 'Imagine – just imagine,' he commanded, 'what would be the wonderful outcome if everyone in town knew of the joy and fellowship of our Sunday mornings in this church.' Nobody else in the choir noticed what the vicar was doing so nobody wakened the bass soloist to imagine the joy and fellowship, and the vicar moved on regardless, saying, 'Yes – quite right. Our church would be bursting at the seams – packed to the rafters.'

He then explained that he had been able to arrange the loan of a builder's lorry and now invited the congregation to form a working party to get down to producing a church float that would be the talk of the town. 'Volunteers now,' he beamed, pointing dramatically to various persons and repeating, 'Jolly good, splendid,' before they had time to think of declining. 'A meeting in the vestry after evensong tonight will be ideal,' he concluded. 'All of us with lots of ideas – for something really *spectacular*.'

Such was the glowing persuasive power of the man that a large number of us who had not actually been nominated as volunteers found ourselves crowded into the vestry with the chosen ones after evensong, where attendance had been at least twice the normal size. He didn't waste time. He opened the meeting by calling immediately for suggestions, but even before he could point to the first volunteer the Any Other Business man was on his feet and in full flood. The AOB man, a huge tweed-clad character with a figure like an all-in wrestler, had been on the church council for ages. He had earned his title from his unfailing habit of having absolutely nothing to say throughout the entire meeting, until late into the night when, all the other members having got thoroughly fed up with arguing with each other and getting nowhere, the last item on the agenda, Any Other Business, was reached. The AOB man would then rise like a prophet of old, fix his gaze firmly above the chairman's head on to a clock with one hand and, using the language of some of his best-loved Victorian hymns, would urge that the church must march as to war and smite its enemies and slay evildoers. This would go on until the chairman could slip in a firm and final expression of thanks for 'those inspiring and indeed much-needed words' and quickly intone the closing prayer.

But at this meeting the AOB man had caught everyone napping. Far from bringing up the rear, he had led the attack. Our float must portray fearless Christian warriors, he declared, vanquishing dragons and evil hordes – and things like that. 'Charge for the God of battles!' he finished triumphantly.

The vicar said, 'Yes, thank you indeed,' and a little lady with a surprisingly commanding voice suggested that friendship and helpfulness should be the theme, and that we should have a float full of teenagers doing things like helping old people cross roads and cleaning risqué graffiti from walls. Her suggestions were followed by a number of others involving healthy eating and drinking and exercise, and one that called for the choir to appear on the float wearing their new plum-coloured cassocks (*'such* a lovely shade') and handing out free surplus parish magazines.

A group of highly respected long-service parishioners, who had always agreed fervently with the views and doings of the old vicar, and now did the same with the new vicar although the outlooks of the two vicars were quite at variance, were very keen that the vicar should appear as St Francis of Assisi.

Jake, who is of a somewhat cynical nature, having dealt intimately with vicars, parochial church councils, and church choirs over many years, summed up by congratulating the gathering on really getting to grips with the subject. 'I can see our float now – clearly!' he exclaimed excitedly. 'All those incredibly heroic warriors smiting and slaying all over the place, while helpful young people are scrubbing the walls and helping old people across the road to the health club, where everybody is doing exercises like mad against a background of lovely plum-coloured cassocks, and St Francis is chatting with the animals and birds because everyone else is too busy or frantic to talk to him . . .'

The vicar thanked Jake for his 'usual and much-enjoyed comic relief' and finally someone had a good idea. It was decided to delay the beginning of the May Fair procession until more of the customers had got out of bed; it was to start at midday. The vicar's builder's lorry failed to materialize, as did a definite theme for the church float, but at the last moment the local brewery came forward with the offer of a horse-drawn dray. The name of the church was strung up above the name of the brewery and the dray hastily loaded with gleeful-looking parishioners who were tickled pink with the idea of substituting for barrels of beer. And the four champion Shire horses that drew the dray also drew by far the most enthusiastic attention from the crowds who surrounded them with batteries of cameras and small children.

There is little that escapes the new vicar's eye when it comes to ideas for filling the pews. He has now taken down the 'NO DOGS' notice in the churchyard and is urgently planning the next great church witness event – a monster animal blessing service. He has already arranged for the choir to arrive in their new plum-coloured cassocks on the brewery horse dray . . .

More Faith

We met quite often on an early morning train to London. We first got into conversation when, to pass the time, we started speculating on why our train was so reluctant to make its way to its destination. It was one of those trains that hang about at each station long after the passengers have alighted and boarded, and then stops for a creaking breather between stations as well. As this procedure continued with dependable regularity the subject became rather stale, our jokes about it repetitive and our empty threats against the railway people boring, and we turned to other topics of conversation. It transpired that my travelling companion was a chorister at a church only a few miles from mine. He was, he said, the lone male alto, known as Hooter, because the choirmaster said he sang like an owl. My enthusiasm to hear about his choir, and his unexpected pleasure in finding someone who understood about stubborn vicars and immovable choirmasters and organists, encouraged him to embark on a regular serial story about the fascinating set-up at his church.

The choir were a constant source of discomfiture to the vicar. Not that they knowingly did anything particularly discomfiting, apart from singing very loud anthems with words taken from the more bloodthirsty passages in the Old Testament, and rendering the vicar's favourite meditative, devotional hymns in the manner of drinking songs in a Bavarian beer cellar. But many a vicar has to put up with similar situations and generally Christian charity or a sense of the inevitable overcomes any angry urges ('Hardly *sensitive* singing – but their *hearts* are in the right place – so loyal, so, er, *enthusiastic*').

However, the case was rather more difficult for this vicar. He was not a good mixer. Despite years of experience he still found it a strain to circulate in the church hall after the Sunday family service and say meaningful things to all the people consuming coffee and biscuits and complaining about the length of the sermon and the last hymn that nobody had ever heard of.

And as for the choir, the very thought of circulating anywhere among, or with, them never failed to fill him with dismay. He was a mild, middle-aged confirmed bachelor, who kept bees and was shy of the choir's young women, terrified of the older, larger ones and looked upon all choirboys as the ultimate test of faith. Only with the men of the choir (when they were well away from the choir) did he find himself at ease. It happened that, like him, they were middle-aged and keen on cricket and gardening. Also they had never put their names forward for membership of the parochial church council or any other committee where people argued with the vicar, asked awkward questions about the church heating system or proposed outlandish ideas for replacing choral evensong.

The vicar fully understood the choirmen's reason for not joining the parochial church council. The PCC was not his favourite organization either, but of course he always had to be at the meetings to keep some kind of order and to hustle the members through the agenda by midnight, or to attempt the near impossible task of getting everyone to agree on a further date when the unfinished arguing could continue.

Doubtless, in view of my interest in the goings-on at his church, Hooter eventually invited me to visit it one Sunday morning and sing in the choir. It was midsummer and, he said, as his choirmaster never gave the slightest consideration to the fact that a large number of the choir were on holiday, and still kept putting on great long anthems and complicated settings, regardless of whether the choir was only half its normal size or had any idea of the music or not, any help in any voice was most welcome. 'We did the Hallelujah Chorus last Sunday with six people in the choir,' Hooter told me, not without a sort of muted pride.

'Handel's Hallelujah Chorus?' I queried.

'Well, yes, that's what it said on the music,' confirmed Hooter, 'but it was mostly *our* Hallelujah Chorus. I told our choirmaster afterwards that Handel wouldn't have recognized it and certainly wouldn't have attempted to perform it with the choir we had.'

'What did he say to that?' I asked.

'Faith,' declared Hooter. 'He said you've got to have faith and then you can move mountains.'

'And put on the Hallelujah Chorus with six people,' I said.

'Well, five really,' he corrected. 'One bloke had forgotten his glasses and couldn't even see the music.'

'Your choirmaster must have a *lot* of faith,' I said admiringly.

'Oh, he has,' Hooter enthused, 'and it pays, you know. I can't remember us ever actually *breaking down*. Whatever mistakes we make, we still go on singing – our choirmaster insists on that. It's part of his faith, y'see. Then the congregation don't even know we've made any slip ups. They've got faith, too. They believe that what they hear us sing is what we are actually supposed to sing.'

Full of interest, but with only a limited amount of faith that I should find Hooter's church (I can lose my way with the greatest of ease crossing the road in unfamiliar territory), I arrived one fine Sunday in August in what I hoped was the right vicinity in plenty of time for morning service. I'm sure that a century ago I would have spotted the red brick Victorian edifice at once, dominating the high street. Now, however, there was no sign of it in the concrete confusion of supermarkets and high-rise office blocks and, it seemed, no one to ask the way. I looked down one or two side streets and studied various signs fixed to lamp-posts, which gave quite a lot of information about the high street bus stop being moved to the railway station, the quickest way to the crematorium and what would happen to you if your dog misbehaved itself on the cracked, rubbish-strewn pavements. But there was nothing about the whereabouts of red brick Victorian churches.

And then appeared a most welcome sight – a man with a boxer dog which, like all boxer dogs, appeared to be grinning from ear to ear and, like all boxer dogs, had a tiny stump of a tail that wagged with such joyous enthusiasm that it convulsed the whole dog. The two of them were on their way to church and were very friendly, particularly the boxer dog, which nearly knocked me over in a frenzy of delight. The man was a churchwarden and the boxer had his own seat in the corner of the back pew. Apparently he was very well behaved during the service – unless the sermon tended to ramble on beyond a reasonable point, whereupon he would rise, stretch and utter a very loud yawn.

The churchwarden conducted me to the choir vestry, which was an unsuspected place behind the organ, full of flower vases and large cardboard boxes containing what looked like rejected jumble sale merchandise. Hooter and the choirmaster stood by a battered piano contemplating the score of a splendidly boisterous festival anthem by Goss of the type that, in its heyday, was sung at the Crystal Palace by choirs of hundreds. Hooter introduced me to the choirmaster who remarked, 'Well, that's one more, then. That means we have a choir of six.'

'Ah,' I said uncertainly.

'That's fine,' said the choirmaster. 'I'll do the bass solo and we'll do the quartet and other solo bits full choir. Right! Fine!' He had a firm, no-nonsense manner and his superior dark suit fitted him like a dress uniform.

A decorative soprano was arranging her appearance before a spotty mirror. 'You'll sing contralto in the Goss,' ordered the choirmaster. 'Flavia's got hay fever.'

'Right,' said the decorative soprano. 'Do I know the Goss?'

'You weren't at choir practice Friday night,' accused the choirmaster.

'I was chasing the vicar,' said the decorative soprano.

'Typical,' said the choirmaster.

'I spotted him in the supermarket,' explained the decorative soprano. 'I'd been trying to get hold of him all week to ask him if we could have the spring fashion show in the vicarage garden next year, but you know what he's like – always out or on the phone.'

'I bet he is when he sees you coming,' observed the choirmaster.

'He saw me and dodged round behind the frozen fish,' recounted the decorative soprano, 'but I cornered him. He started blushing and stuttering and I got him to lend us the garden *and* promise to open the show. It took me ages, though. So I didn't get to practice.'

'Good heavens!' gasped the choirmaster. 'Do you really imagine he'll actually do it?'

'It's like you are always saying about the choir.' She beamed a bewitching smile at the choirmaster. 'You've got to have faith.'

Well, Sir John Goss would, I am sure, have appreciated the faith our semi-demolished choir needed to get through his splendid anthem that we sang that evening, 'The Wilderness'. Goss, a distinguished nineteenth-century organist of St Paul's Cathedral, had to have the same faith, to a much greater degree, in order to produce the required singing from the ramshackle crowd that in his day were known as the cathedral choir. Sir John would have been pleased with us, I think. We didn't break down.

Faith was strong in the air. I learned some months later from Hooter that even the vicar found some. The decorative soprano *did* make sure that he opened the spring fashion show, and to his surprise he enjoyed himself so much being consulted on his fashion ideas by so many charming people that he had put himself forward to open the next year's show. And he finds chatting over coffee after Sunday morning service much easier now. Not that he approaches it with unqualified enthusiasm even so, for whereas the fashion show people politely, indeed charmingly, asked his opinions, the church crowd pin him in corners before he can even get to the coffee counter, and tell him why they don't agree with him and what they are going to do about it. Still, it's a beginning, and as the choirmaster says, 'You've got to have faith and then you can move mountains.'